MW00932433

MacBook Pro User Guide

Manual for Beginners and Seniors on
How to Use MacBook Pro
(2022 Edition)

Steve Rufus

Contents

Introducing the new 14-inch and 16-inch MacBook Pro 6

Introducing the new 14-inch and 16-inch MacBook Pro...............6

MacBook Pro at a glance 7

Take a tour: 13-inch MacBook Pro 9

What's included: 14-inch and 16-inch MacBook Pro 11

What's included: 13-inch MacBook Pro.....................................14

Magic Keyboard for 14-inch and 16-inch MacBook Pro.............15

Magic Keyboard for 13-inch MacBook Pro 18

13-inch MacBook Pro: Use the Touch Bar 21

13-inch MacBook Pro: Customize the Touch Bar 24

MacBook Pro trackpad..25

Charge the MacBook Pro battery 27

MacBook Pro accessories...29

Work with wireless accessories...30

Use an external display with your MacBook Pro.........................31

Set up your MacBook Pro...34

Apple Account on Mac 37

Find your way around...41

The Finder on your Mac 43

13-inch MacBook Pro: Use the Finder with the Touch Bar 46

The Dock on your Mac..47

Notification Center on your Mac 48

System Preferences on your Mac 52

Spotlight on your Mac 53

Siri on your Mac...55

Window management on your Mac...57

Display settings for your Mac 59

Transfer your data to your new MacBook Pro........................... 61

Back up and restore your Mac................................... 62

Accessibility on your Mac 63

New features on your MacBook Pro............................... 69

Use MacBook Pro with other devices............................... 73

Use your MacBook Pro with iCloud and Continuity.................... 73

Access your iCloud content on your Mac........................... 74

Screen Time on Mac 77

Use Handoff on your Mac... 78

Use Universal Clipboard on your Mac 79

Sidecar on your Mac 80

Continuity Camera on your Mac 82

Continuity Sketch and Continuity Markup on your Mac.............. 84

Use AirDrop on your Mac 85

Phone calls and text messages on your Mac........................ 87

Instant Hotspot on your Mac..................................... 88

Unlock your Mac and approve tasks with Apple Watch 89

Use Apple Pay on your Mac...................................... 91

Use AirPlay on your Mac... 93

Use AirPrint on your Mac 94

Apps 96

Apps on your MacBook Pro...................................... 96

App Store 99

Books.. 102

Calendar 105

FaceTime 108

Find My 110

GarageBand 112

Home 114

iMovie 116

Keynote.. 118

Mail 120

Maps.. 124

Messages 126

Music 131

News.. 133

Notes 135

Numbers 139

Pages 141

Photos 144

Podcasts.. 148

Preview... 151

Reminders 152

Safari 154

Shortcuts.. 160

Stocks.. 163

TV 165

Voice Memos 166

Find answers 169

Use the macOS User Guide.................................... 169

Are you new to Mac? 171

Keyboard shortcuts on your Mac............................ 174

Security features on your MacBook Pro 176

Save space on your MacBook Pro 176

Take a screenshot on your Mac 178

Introducing the new 14-inch and 16-inch MacBook Pro

Introducing the new 14-inch and 16-inch MacBook Pro

The new 14-inch and 16-inch models of MacBook Pro deliver extraordinary pro performance and amazing battery life, thanks to the power and efficiency of Apple silicon. These models feature a Liquid Retina XDR display for a stunning front-of-screen experience and a versatile array of ports for pro connectivity. They also have a 1080p FaceTime HD camera, a high-fidelity six-speaker sound system, and a studio-quality three-mic array that together enable great video calls.

See it all on your bold and bright display

The Liquid Retina XDR display delivers extreme dynamic range, high contrast ratio, adaptive refresh rates, and advanced color accuracy. Everyone will enjoy the vivid quality, whether they're grading 8K video on-set, or watching a movie in HDR to get a truly cinematic experience.

Use all the functionality on your keyboard

The Magic Keyboard includes a row of full-height function keys with new keyboard shortcuts for Spotlight search 🔍, Siri/Dictation 🎤, and Do Not Disturb 🌙, which allow you to quickly focus on the task at hand.

Connect all your devices

The new MacBook Pro models have versatile connectivity—including three Thunderbolt 4 (USB-C) ports, an HDMI port, an SDXC card slot, a MagSafe 3 port for the power adapter, and a 3.5 mm headphone jack that supports high-impedance headphones—so you can connect and use all your devices easily.

Charge quickly and safely

Connect the USB-C to MagSafe 3 Cable to the power adapter and the MagSafe 3 port. As the connector gets close to the port, you'll feel a magnetic pull drawing it in. With the 96W USB-C Power Adapter for the 14-inch model and the 140W USB-C Power Adapter for the 16-inch model, MacBook Pro can be charged up to 50 percent in about 30 minutes.

MacBook Pro at a glance

Take a tour: New 14-inch and 16-inch MacBook Pro

Note: This guide is for the currently shipping MacBook Pro models. The 14-inch and 16-inch MacBook Pro models have the following features. Not all features are available on all MacBook Pro models.

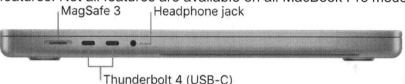

- **MagSafe 3 port**: Plug in the included USB-C Power Adapter to recharge the MacBook Pro battery. The indicator light glows amber when the battery needs to be charged, and green when it's fully charged. Charge your battery quickly— up to 50 percent in 30 minutes—on the 14-inch model with the 96W USB-C Power Adapter, and on the 16-inch model with the 140W USB-C Power Adapter.
- **Thunderbolt 4 (USB-C) ports**: Transfer data at Thunderbolt speeds (up to 40 Gbps), connect to a display or projector, connect to USB 4 peripherals, and more.
- **3.5 mm headphone jack**: Plug in stereo headphones or external speakers to listen to your favorite music or movies. Use high-impedance headphones without a digital-to-analog converter or an amplifier.

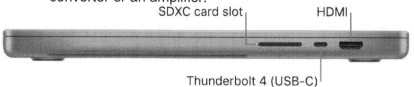

- **SDXC card slot**: Transfer photos, videos, and data to and from your MacBook Pro, with support for high-capacity SD 4.0 cards.
- **HDMI port**: Connect your MacBook Pro to a TV or external display.

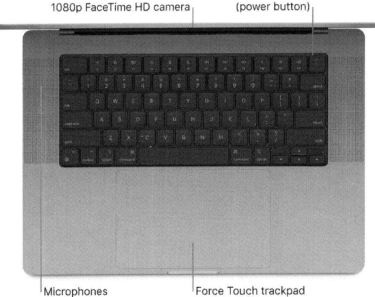

1080p FaceTime HD camera

Touch ID (power button)

Microphones

Force Touch trackpad

- **1080p FaceTime HD camera**: Make FaceTime video calls or take pictures and video. The camera system provides high-quality video and better low-light performance. If the green indicator light next to the camera is glowing, the camera is on.
- **Studio-Quality Microphones**: Three microphones with high signal-to-noise ratio and directional beamforming deliver super-clear audio for videoconferencing and phone calls, as well as high-quality voice recordings for audio tracks, podcasts, and voice memos.
- **Speakers**: The high-fidelity six-speaker sound system consists of two pairs of dual force-canceling woofers and two tweeters. Enjoy a robust and high-quality audio experience, including spatial audio support for videos and songs with Dolby Atmos.
- **Touch ID (the power button)**: Press to turn on your MacBook Pro (or just lift the lid or press any key). A metallic trim ring guides your finger to the Touch ID sensor that

analyzes your fingerprint. When you first start up or restart, you need to log in by typing your password.
- **Force Touch trackpad**: Control your MacBook Pro with gestures. The entire trackpad surface acts as a button so you can easily click anywhere.

Take a tour: 13-inch MacBook Pro

Note: This guide is for the currently shipping MacBook Pro models.

The 13-inch MacBook Pro with M1 chip has the following features. Not all features are available on all MacBook Pro models.

Thunderbolt 4 (USB-C)

- **Thunderbolt / USB 4 port**: Charge your computer, transfer data at Thunderbolt speeds (up to 40 Gbps), connect to a display or projector, USB 4 peripherals, and more.

Headphone jack

- **3.5 mm headphone jack**: Plug in stereo headphones or external speakers to listen to your favorite music or movies.

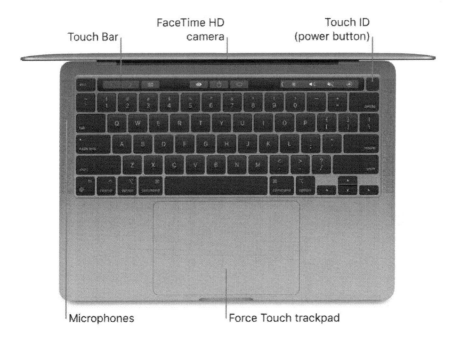

Touch Bar   FaceTime HD camera   Touch ID (power button)

Microphones   Force Touch trackpad

- **Microphones**: Record live music, make conference calls, and mix audio on the go. The three-microphone array on the MacBook Pro delivers studio-quality recordings with high signal-to-noise ratio and directional beamforming.
- **Touch Bar**: The Touch Bar at the top of the keyboard dynamically adapts to the app you're using. The Touch Bar is an extension of the keyboard—it presents intuitive shortcuts and application controls, when and where you need them. You can use familiar gestures like swipe and tap in the Touch Bar.
- **FaceTime HD camera**: Make FaceTime video calls or take pictures and video. If the light is glowing, the camera is on.
- **Touch ID (the power button)**: Press to turn on your MacBook Pro (or just lift the lid or press any key). When you first start up or restart, you need to log in by typing your password.
- **Force Touch trackpad**: Control your MacBook Pro with gestures. The entire trackpad surface acts as a button so you can easily click anywhere.

What's included: 14-inch and 16-inch MacBook Pro

To use your MacBook Pro, you need a power adapter and a cable, included in the box:

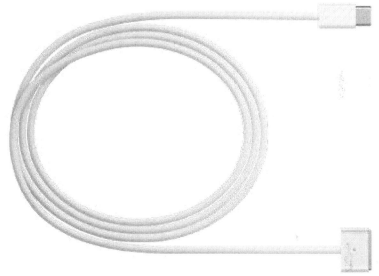

- **USB-C to MagSafe 3 Cable**: To charge your MacBook Pro, connect one end of the USB-C to MagSafe 3 Cable to the MagSafe 3 port on your MacBook Pro, and the other end to the power adapter (67W USB-C Power Adapter, 96W USB-C Power Adapter, or 140W USB-C Power Adapter). When you first connect the cable to MacBook Pro, an indicator on the connector starts to glow, indicating battery status: green for fully charged or amber for charging.

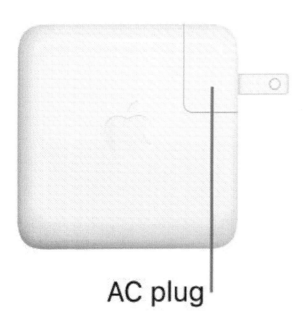

AC plug

- **67W USB-C Power Adapter or 96W USB-C Power Adapter**: After the power adapter is connected, fully extend the electrical prongs on the AC plug, and plug the adapter into an AC power outlet. The 96W USB-C Power Adapter for the 14-inch MacBook Pro fast charges MacBook Pro to approximately 50 percent in about 30 minutes.

AC plug

- **140W USB-C Power Adapter**: After the power adapter is connected, fully extend the electrical prongs on the AC plug, and plug the adapter into an AC power outlet. The 140W USB-C Power Adapter for the 16-inch MacBook Pro fast charges MacBook Pro to approximately 50 percent in about 30 minutes.

Automatically start up your MacBook Pro. Use the USB-C to MagSafe 3 Cable to connect your MacBook Pro to the power adapter (67W USB-C Power Adapter, 96W USB-C Power Adapter, or 140W USB-C Power Adapter), then plug in the power adapter. Lift the lid and touch any key to turn on and start up your MacBook Pro. Log in and get right to work.

Other adapters and accessories are sold separately. Visit apple.com, your local Apple Store, or other resellers for more information and availability. Review the documentation or check with the manufacturer to make sure you choose the right product.

What's included: 13-inch MacBook Pro

To use your MacBook Pro, you need these two accessories, included in the box:

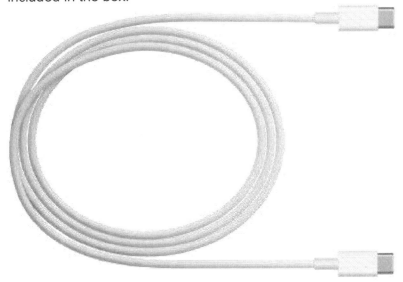

- **USB-C Charge Cable**: To charge your MacBook Pro, connect one end of the USB-C Charge Cable to any Thunderbolt port on your MacBook Pro, and the other end to the 61W USB-C Power Adapter.

AC plug

- **61W USB-C Power Adapter**: After the power adapter is connected, fully extend the electrical prongs on the AC plug, and plug the adapter into an AC power outlet.

Automatically start up your MacBook Pro. Connect your 61W USB-C Power Adapter and USB-C Charge Cable and lift the lid and touch any key to turn on and start up your MacBook Pro. Log in and get right to work.

Other adapters and accessories are sold separately. Visit apple.com, your local Apple Store, or other resellers for more information and availability. Review the documentation or check with the manufacturer to make sure you choose the right product.

Magic Keyboard for 14-inch and 16-inch MacBook Pro

The function keys on the top row of the Magic Keyboard on your 14-inch and 16-inch MacBook Pro provide shortcuts for common functions, such as increasing the volume or screen brightness.

Touch ID (the power button) is located on the right side of the function keys. After you set up Touch ID, you can use your fingerprint to unlock MacBook Pro, quickly lock your screen, or make purchases from the App Store, Apple TV app, and Apple Books, and on websites using Apple Pay.

You can set up Touch ID during setup, or later in the Touch ID pane of System Preferences. To set keyboard preferences, open System Preferences, click Keyboard, then click the buttons at the top to see the available options.

Touch ID (power button)

Function (Fn)/Globe key

Use Touch ID (the power button). Press to turn on your MacBook Pro (or just lift the lid and press any key). When you first start up or restart the computer, you need to log in by typing your password. After setup and initial login, whenever you're asked for your password in the same session, you can just place your finger lightly on the Touch ID sensor to authenticate.
Press the Touch ID key to quickly lock your screen.

You can also use Touch ID to make online purchases securely with Apple Pay.

Note: To turn off your MacBook Pro, choose Apple menu > Shut

Down. To put your MacBook Pro to sleep, choose Apple menu
> Sleep.

16

Many system functions can be accessed through the function keys.

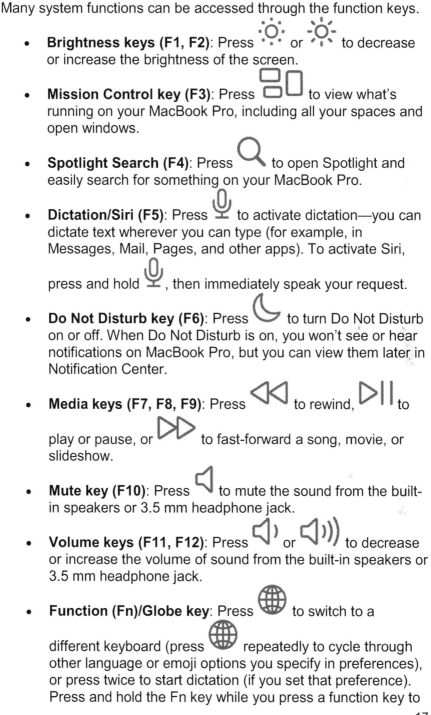

- **Brightness keys (F1, F2)**: Press ⟨symbol⟩ or ⟨symbol⟩ to decrease or increase the brightness of the screen.

- **Mission Control key (F3)**: Press ⟨symbol⟩ to view what's running on your MacBook Pro, including all your spaces and open windows.

- **Spotlight Search (F4)**: Press ⟨symbol⟩ to open Spotlight and easily search for something on your MacBook Pro.

- **Dictation/Siri (F5)**: Press ⟨symbol⟩ to activate dictation—you can dictate text wherever you can type (for example, in Messages, Mail, Pages, and other apps). To activate Siri, press and hold ⟨symbol⟩, then immediately speak your request.

- **Do Not Disturb key (F6)**: Press ⟨symbol⟩ to turn Do Not Disturb on or off. When Do Not Disturb is on, you won't see or hear notifications on MacBook Pro, but you can view them later in Notification Center.

- **Media keys (F7, F8, F9)**: Press ⟨symbol⟩ to rewind, ⟨symbol⟩ to play or pause, or ⟨symbol⟩ to fast-forward a song, movie, or slideshow.

- **Mute key (F10)**: Press ⟨symbol⟩ to mute the sound from the built-in speakers or 3.5 mm headphone jack.

- **Volume keys (F11, F12)**: Press ⟨symbol⟩ or ⟨symbol⟩ to decrease or increase the volume of sound from the built-in speakers or 3.5 mm headphone jack.

- **Function (Fn)/Globe key**: Press ⟨symbol⟩ to switch to a different keyboard (press ⟨symbol⟩ repeatedly to cycle through other language or emoji options you specify in preferences), or press twice to start dictation (if you set that preference). Press and hold the Fn key while you press a function key to trigger the action associated with the key. Each function key on the top row can also perform other functions—for example, the F11 key can hide all open windows and show the desktop.

To specify options for the Function (Fn)/Globe key, open System Preferences, click Keyboard, and choose options to change your keyboard or input source, show emoji and symbols, start dictation, or define functions.

Learn about keyboard shortcuts. You can press key combinations to do things on your MacBook Pro that you'd normally do with a trackpad, mouse, or other device. For example, press Command-C to copy selected text, then click where you want to paste the text and press Command-V.

Magic Keyboard for 13-inch MacBook Pro

The Touch Bar at the top of the Magic Keyboard on the 13-inch MacBook Pro displays a set of tools that changes based on what you're doing. Touch ID (the power button) is located on the right side of the Touch Bar. After you set up Touch ID, you can use your fingerprint to unlock MacBook Pro, quickly lock your screen, or make purchases from the App Store, Apple TV app, and Apple Books, and on websites using Apple Pay.

You can set up Touch ID during setup, or later in the Touch ID pane of System Preferences. To set keyboard and Touch Bar preferences, open System Preferences, click Keyboard, then click the buttons at the top to see the available options.

Touch Bar

Touch ID (power button)

Function (Fn)/Globe key

Use Touch ID (the power button). Press to turn on your MacBook Pro (or just lift the lid and press any key). When you first start up or restart the computer, you need to log in by typing your password. After setup and initial login, whenever you're asked for your password in the same session, you can just place your finger lightly on the Touch ID sensor to authenticate.

Press the Touch ID sensor to quickly lock your MacBook Pro screen.

You can also use Touch ID to make secure online purchases with Apple Pay.

Note: To turn off your MacBook Pro, choose Apple menu > Shut

Down. To put your MacBook Pro to sleep, choose Apple menu > Sleep.

All system functions are located on the Touch Bar.

- **Brightness buttons**: Press or to decrease or increase the brightness of the screen.

- **Mission Control button**: Press to view what's running on your MacBook Pro, including all your spaces and open windows.

19

- **Launchpad button**: Press 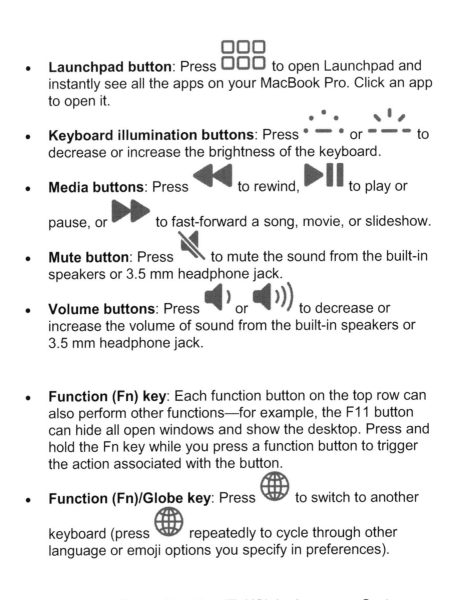 to open Launchpad and instantly see all the apps on your MacBook Pro. Click an app to open it.

- **Keyboard illumination buttons**: Press or to decrease or increase the brightness of the keyboard.

- **Media buttons**: Press to rewind, to play or pause, or to fast-forward a song, movie, or slideshow.

- **Mute button**: Press to mute the sound from the built-in speakers or 3.5 mm headphone jack.

- **Volume buttons**: Press or to decrease or increase the volume of sound from the built-in speakers or 3.5 mm headphone jack.

- **Function (Fn) key**: Each function button on the top row can also perform other functions—for example, the F11 button can hide all open windows and show the desktop. Press and hold the Fn key while you press a function button to trigger the action associated with the button.

- **Function (Fn)/Globe key**: Press to switch to another keyboard (press repeatedly to cycle through other language or emoji options you specify in preferences).

To specify options for the Function (Fn)/Globe key, open System Preferences, click Keyboard, and choose options to change your keyboard or input source, show emoji and symbols, start dictation, or define functions.

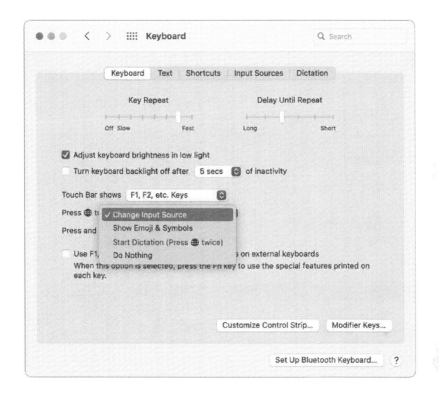

Learn about keyboard shortcuts. You can press key combinations to do things on your MacBook Pro that you'd normally do with a trackpad, mouse, or other device. For example, press Command-C to copy selected text, then click where you want to paste the text and press Command-V.

13-inch MacBook Pro: Use the Touch Bar

The Touch Bar on the 13-inch MacBook Pro is integrated into many macOS apps to give you handy shortcuts for the tasks you do most, based on your current app and activity. Use familiar gestures—like tap and swipe—in the Touch Bar while you work.

The buttons at the right end of the Touch Bar are the Control Strip— you use them to expand or collapse the Control Strip, change the brightness and volume, or activate Siri. The other buttons in the Touch Bar depend on the app you're using.

Tap to expand
the Control Strip.

These buttons are
always available.

Expand or collapse the Control Strip. Frequently used system controls, like volume and brightness, are located in the Control Strip on the right side of the Touch Bar. Tap 〈 to expand the strip, then tap buttons or sliders for the settings you want to change. Tap ⊗ when you finish, or leave the Control Strip open to keep the buttons available.

Customize the Control Strip. Click Keyboard in System Preferences, then click Customize Control Strip. Drag controls to the bottom of your screen and into the Touch Bar to add them. In Keyboard Preferences, you can also select options for what the Control Strip displays—for example, function keys or desktop spaces.

Display the function keys. Press and hold the Function (Fn) key to display the function keys F1 through F12 in the Touch Bar, then tap a function button to use it.

Use the Esc button. The Esc button usually appears on the left side of the Touch Bar, in the same place the Esc key appears on traditional keyboards. Esc appears on the left even when the other tools on the Touch Bar change.

Tap instead of type. In apps where you compose text, like Notes, Messages, TextEdit, and Mail, the Touch Bar can display typing suggestions to help you save time by presenting words and emoji you can tap instead of type. Tap  in the Touch Bar to see typing suggestions, if they're not already showing.

Note: Typing suggestions may not be available in all languages or in all areas.

Express yourself with emoji. In some apps, you can choose an emoji instead of words for a fun way to make your point. Tap to display the emoji. Swipe to scroll through options, organized by category, such as "Frequently Used," "Smileys & People," "Travel & Places," and more. Tap to select the emoji you want.

Explore and experiment. Tap around to see what you can accomplish quickly and efficiently. It's often easier to tap the Touch Bar than to click or select items onscreen in order to accomplish a task or apply a setting. For example, open Calculator and do quick calculations with the number keys and the functions on the Touch Bar—no more moving your pointer, clicking, and typing onscreen.

Keep using the Touch Bar to find the best ways to achieve the results you want. Move seamlessly between the Touch Bar, your keyboard, and the trackpad to get the job done.

13-inch MacBook Pro: Customize the Touch Bar

Customize the Touch Bar on the 13-inch MacBook Pro

In the Finder and in apps such as Mail and Safari, you can customize the buttons in the Touch Bar. You can also customize the Control Strip. Choose View > Customize Touch Bar to add, delete, or rearrange items in the Touch Bar.

When you're customizing the Touch Bar, the buttons jiggle. For example, here's the Calculator Touch Bar, ready to be edited:

Add buttons to the Touch Bar. Drag controls to the bottom of your screen and into the Touch Bar to add them.

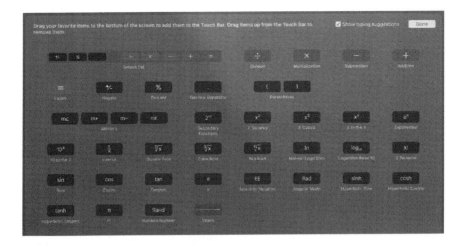

When you finish, click Done on the screen.

Rearrange buttons in the Touch Bar. While customizing the Touch Bar, drag buttons to a new location. When you finish, click Done on the screen.

Remove buttons from the Touch Bar. While customizing the Touch Bar, drag a button from the Touch Bar to the screen to remove it. When you finish, click Done on the screen.

MacBook Pro trackpad

You can do a lot on your MacBook Pro using simple trackpad gestures—scroll through webpages, zoom in on documents, rotate photos, and more. With the Force Touch trackpad, pressure-sensing capabilities add another level of interactivity. The trackpad provides feedback—when you drag or rotate objects, you feel a subtle vibration when they're aligned, allowing you to work with greater precision.

Here are some common gestures:

Gesture	Action
●	**Click**: Press anywhere on the trackpad. Or enable "Tap to click" in Trackpad preferences, and simply tap.
◎	**Force click**: Click and then press deeper. You can use force click to look up more information— click a word to see its definition, or an address to see a preview that you can open in Maps.
●●	**Secondary click (that is, right-click)**: Click with two fingers to open shortcut menus. If "Tap to click" is enabled, tap with two fingers. On the keyboard, press the Control key and click the trackpad.

	Two-finger scroll: Slide two fingers up or down to scroll.
	Pinch to zoom: Pinch your thumb and finger open or closed to zoom in or out of photos and webpages.
	Swipe to navigate: Swipe left or right with two fingers to flip through webpages, documents, and more—like turning a page in a book.
	Open Launchpad: Quickly open apps in Launchpad. Pinch closed with four or five fingers, then click an app to open it.
	Swipe between apps: To switch from one full-screen app to another, swipe left or right with three or four fingers.

Customize your gestures. In System Preferences, click Trackpad. You can do the following:

- Learn more about each gesture
- Set the click pressure you prefer to use
- Decide whether to use pressure-sensing features
- Customize other trackpad features

Tip: If you find you're force clicking when you don't intend to, try adjusting the click pressure to a firmer setting in Trackpad preferences. Or change the "Look up & data detectors" option from the "Force Click with one finger" default setting to "Tap with three fingers."

Charge the MacBook Pro battery

The battery in your MacBook Pro recharges whenever the MacBook Pro is connected to power, unless you have options set.

Charge the battery. Connect your 13-inch MacBook Pro to a power outlet using the included USB-C Charge Cable and 61W USB-C Power Adapter.

Connect your 14-inch or 16-inch MacBook Pro to a power outlet using the included 67W USB-C Power Adapter, 96W USB-C Power Adapter, or 140W USB-C Power Adapter and USB-C to MagSafe 3 Cable.

You can set options in the Battery pane of System Preferences:

- **Slightly dim the display while on battery power**: Keeps your display dimmed to save energy while you're using battery power.
- **Automatic graphics switching**: Your MacBook Pro will automatically choose the best graphics mode based on your usage to increase battery life.
- **Optimize video streaming while on battery**: This is not on by default, but you might want to turn it on while doing a presentation.
- **Show battery status in menu bar**: Adds an icon to the status bar so you can quickly see information about your battery and open Battery Preferences.
- **Optimized Battery Charging**: This feature helps to reduce the wear on your battery and improve its lifespan by learning

your daily charging routine. It delays charging the battery past 80% when it predicts that you'll be plugged in for an extended period of time, and aims to charge the battery before you unplug. You can change this option in Battery preferences.

- **Low Power Mode**: This option reduces energy usage and increases battery life. This is a good option for travel or when you're away from a power source for an extended period of time.
- **High Power Mode**: Available on the 16-inch MacBook Pro with Apple M1 Max. When selected, your Mac allows the fans to run at higher speeds to maximize performance during intensive workloads.

To charge the battery, use the MagSafe 3 port or any of the Thunderbolt 4 (USB-C) ports on your 14-inch or 16-inch MacBook Pro, or any of the Thunderbolt / USB 4 ports on your 13-inch MacBook Pro.

Check the battery's charge. Look at the battery status icon at the right of the menu bar to see the battery level or charging status.

Charging   Charged

Battery usage history. Click Battery in System Preferences, then click Usage History to see your battery's usage over the past 24 hours or the last 10 days.

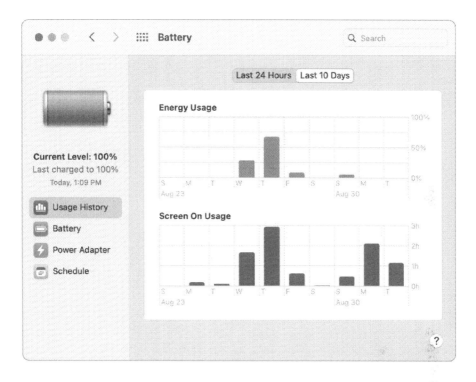

Conserve battery power. To extend battery life on a given charge, you can reduce the display brightness, close apps, and disconnect peripheral devices you're not using. Click Battery in System Preferences to change your power settings. If your MacBook Pro is in sleep when a device is connected to it, the device's battery may drain.

MacBook Pro accessories

The following Apple accessories are available to connect your MacBook Pro to power, external devices and displays, and more.

Cable or Adapter	Description
	USB-C to USB Adapter: Connect your MacBook Pro to standard USB accessories.

	USB-C to Lightning Cable: Connect your iPhone or other iOS or iPadOS device to your MacBook Pro for syncing and charging.
	USB-C Digital AV Multiport Adapter: Connect your MacBook Pro to an HDMI display, while also connecting a standard USB device and a USB-C charge cable to charge your MacBook Pro. Connect directly to the HDMI port on the 14-inch and 16-inch MacBook Pro.
	USB-C VGA Multiport Adapter: Connect your MacBook Pro to a VGA projector or display, while also connecting a standard USB device and a USB-C charge cable to charge your MacBook Pro.
	Thunderbolt 3 (USB-C) to Thunderbolt 2 Adapter: Connect your MacBook Pro to Thunderbolt 2 devices.

Work with wireless accessories

Using Bluetooth® technology, your MacBook Pro can wirelessly connect (that is, pair) with devices such as a Bluetooth keyboard, mouse, trackpad, headset, wearable sport accessory, and more.

Connect a Bluetooth device. Turn on the device so that it's discoverable, then open System Preferences and click Bluetooth.

Select the device in the list, then click Connect. The device remains connected until you remove it. Control-click a device name to remove it.

Turn Bluetooth on or off. Click the Control Center icon ⬤ in the menu bar, click the Bluetooth icon ✽, then click the control to turn Bluetooth on or off. If you have the Bluetooth ✽ icon in your menu bar, you can click that and then turn the control on or off. Your MacBook Pro comes with Bluetooth turned on.

Tip: If you don't see the Bluetooth icon ✽ in the menu bar, you can add it. Click the Bluetooth icon ✽ in Control Center, click Bluetooth Preferences, then select "Show Bluetooth in menu bar.

Use an external display with your MacBook Pro

You can use an external display, a projector, or an HDTV with your 14-inch or 16-inch MacBook Pro. The HDMI and Thunderbolt ports on your MacBook Pro support video output. You can connect up to two external displays with up to 6K resolution at 60Hz (Apple M1 Pro) or up to three external displays with up to 6K resolution and one external display with up to 4K resolution at 60Hz (Apple M1 Max).

You can use an external display, a projector, or an HDTV with your 13-inch MacBook Pro. The Thunderbolt ports on your MacBook Pro support video output.

- **Connect a VGA display or projector**: Use a USB-C VGA Multiport Adapter to connect the display or projector to a Thunderbolt port on your MacBook Pro.
- **Connect an HDMI display or HDTV**: Plug a cable from your HDMI display or HDTV directly into the HDMI port on your 14-inch or 16-inch MacBook Pro. Use a USB-C Digital AV Multiport Adapter to connect the HDMI display or HDTV to a Thunderbolt / USB 4 port on your 13-inch MacBook Pro.
- **Connect a USB-C display**: Connect the display to a Thunderbolt port on your MacBook Pro.

Note: The MacBook Pro can support full 6K resolution on the Apple Pro Display XDR.
If your display has a connector that doesn't match the port you want to use, you may be able to use it with an adapter (sold separately). Visit apple.com, your local Apple Store, or other resellers for more information and availability. Review the display's documentation or check with the display's manufacturer to make sure you choose the right product.

Tip: If you have an HDTV connected to an Apple TV, you can use AirPlay to mirror your MacBook Pro screen on your TV screen in up to 1080p HD.

Adjust and arrange displays. After you connect an external display or projector, use Displays preferences in System Preferences to set how the displays are arranged, turn screen mirroring on or off, and make other adjustments to color, resolution, and more.

Troubleshooting. If you're not sure how many external displays your MacBook Pro supports, check the Resources tab in About This Mac.

Choose Apple menu > About This Mac > Resources, click Specifications, then locate Video Support (you may need to scroll).

Set up your MacBook Pro

The first time your MacBook Pro starts up, Setup Assistant walks you through the simple steps needed to start using your new Mac. You can respond to all the prompts, or skip some steps and choose to complete them later. For example, it might make sense to set up Screen Time—which you can set for different users—after initial setup.

Setup Assistant guides you through the following:

- **Set your country or region**: This sets the language and time zone for your Mac.
  - **Accessibility options**: View accessibility options for Vision, Motor, Hearing, Cognitive abilities, or click Not Now.

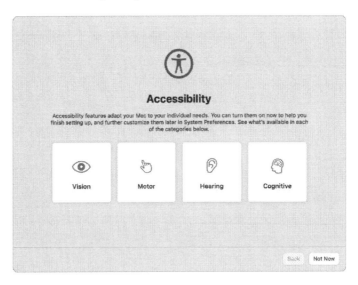

- **Connect to a Wi-Fi network**: Choose the network and enter a password, if necessary. (If you're using Ethernet, you can also choose Other Network Options.) To change the network later, click the Wi-Fi status icon in the menu bar or in Control Center, click Other Networks, then choose a Wi-Fi network and enter the password. You can also choose to turn Wi-Fi on or off here.

Tip: After setup, if you don't see the Wi-Fi status icon in the menu bar, you can add it. Open System Preferences, then click Network. Click Wi-Fi in the list on the left, then select "Show Wi-Fi status in menu bar."

- **Transfer information**: If you're setting up a new computer and you haven't previously set up a Mac, click Not Now in the Migration Assistant window.

- **Sign in with your Apple ID**: Your Apple ID consists of an email address and a password. It's the account you use for everything you do with Apple—including using the App Store, Apple TV app, Apple Books, iCloud, Messages, and more. It's best to have your own Apple ID and not share it. If you don't already have an Apple ID, you can create one during setup (it's free). Sign in with the same Apple ID to use any Apple service, on any device—whether it's your computer, iOS device, iPadOS device, or Apple Watch.

Tip: If you've already set up another device with the latest software versions (macOS 12 or later, iOS 15 or later, iPadOS 15 or later), you'll see a panel for express setup, "Make This Your new Mac," that skips a lot of the steps and uses the settings stored in your iCloud account.

- **Store files in iCloud**: With iCloud, you can store your content—documents, photos, and more—in the cloud, and access it anywhere you go. Be sure to sign in with the same Apple ID on all your devices. To set this option later, open System Preferences and sign in with your Apple ID if you haven't already. Click Apple ID, click iCloud in the sidebar, then select the features you want to use. You can also choose to use iCloud Keychain to save your passwords during setup.

- **Screen Time**: Monitor and get reports on the use of your computer.

- **Enable Siri and "Hey Siri"**: You can turn on Siri and "Hey Siri" (so you can speak your Siri requests) during setup. To enable "Hey Siri," speak several Siri commands when prompted.

- **Set up Touch ID**: You can add a fingerprint to Touch ID during setup. To set up Touch ID later, or to add additional fingerprints, open System Preferences, then click Touch ID.

  To add a fingerprint, click ╋ and follow the onscreen instructions.

  You can also set options for how you want to use Touch ID on your MacBook Pro: to unlock your Mac, use Apple Pay, purchase items on the App Store, Apple TV app, Apple Books, and websites, and auto-fill your password.

Tip: If two or more users use the same MacBook Pro, each user can add a fingerprint to Touch ID to quickly unlock, authenticate, and log in to the MacBook Pro. You can add up to three fingerprints per user account, and a total of five fingerprints for all your MacBook Pro user accounts.

- **Set up Apple Pay**: You can set up Apple Pay for one user account on your MacBook Pro during setup. Other users can still pay with Apple Pay, but they must complete the purchase using their iPhone or Apple Watch that's been set up for Apple Pay. Follow the onscreen prompts to add and verify your card. If you already use a card for media purchases, you might be prompted to verify this card first.

To set up Apple Pay or add additional cards later, open System Preferences, then click Wallet & Apple Pay. Follow the onscreen prompts to set up Apple Pay.

Note: The card issuer determines whether your card is eligible to use with Apple Pay, and may ask you to provide additional information to complete the verification process. Many credit and debit cards can be used with Apple Pay.

- **Choose your look**: Select Light, Dark, or Auto for your desktop appearance. If you want to change the choice you make during setup, open System Preferences, click General, then select an appearance option. You can also set other preferences here.

Apple Account on Mac

Your Apple ID is an account that lets you access all Apple services. Use your Apple ID to download apps from the App Store; access media in Apple Music, Apple Podcasts, Apple TV, and Apple Books; keep your content up to date across devices using iCloud; set up a Family Sharing group; and more.

You can also use your Apple ID to access other apps and websites.

Important: If you forget your Apple ID password, you don't need to create a new Apple ID. Just click the "Forgot Apple ID or password?" link in the sign-in window to retrieve your password.

If other family members use Apple devices, make sure that each family member has their own Apple ID. You can create Apple ID accounts for your kids and share purchases and subscriptions with Family Sharing, described later in this section.

All in one place. Manage everything related to your Apple ID in the same place. Open System Preferences on your MacBook Pro—your Apple ID and Family Sharing settings are at the top.

Turn iCloud on or off.

Update account information.

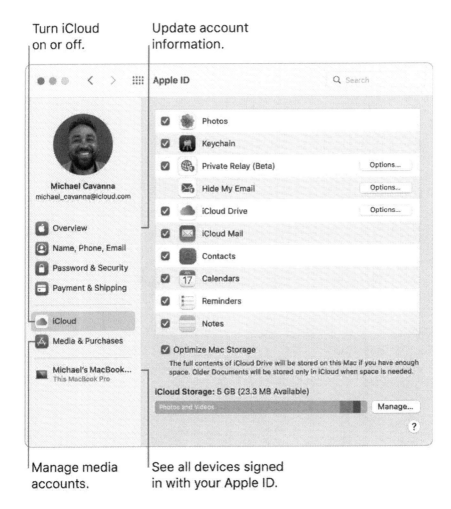

Manage media accounts.

See all devices signed in with your Apple ID.

Update account, security, and payment information. In System Preferences, click Apple ID, then select an item in the sidebar to review and update the information associated with your account.

- **Overview**: The Overview pane lets you know if your account is set up and working properly—if not, you see tips and notifications here.
- **Name, Phone, Email**: Update the name and contact information associated with your Apple ID. You can also manage Apple email newsletter subscriptions.
- **Password & Security**: Change your Apple ID password, turn on two-factor authentication, add or remove trusted

phone numbers, and generate verification codes to sign in to another device or iCloud.com. You can also manage which apps and websites use Sign in with Apple.

- **Payment & Shipping**: Manage the payment methods affiliated with your Apple ID, and your shipping address for purchases from the Apple Store.
- **iCloud**: Select the checkbox next to an iCloud feature to turn the feature on. When you turn on an iCloud feature, your content is stored in iCloud and not locally on your Mac, so you can access any content on any device with iCloud turned on and signed in with the same Apple ID.
- **Media & Purchases**: Manage the accounts linked to Apple Music, Apple Podcasts, Apple TV, and Apple Books; select purchasing settings; and manage your subscriptions.

See all your devices. At the bottom of the Apple ID sidebar, see all the devices linked to your Apple ID. You can verify that Find My [device] is turned on for each one, see the status of iCloud Backup for an iOS or iPadOS device, or remove a device from your account if you no longer own it.

Family Sharing. With Family Sharing, you can set up a family group and create Apple ID accounts for your kids. To manage your family sharing settings, click Family Sharing in System Preferences and select an icon in the sidebar to review and update your information. You can add or remove family members; share media purchases, payment methods, iCloud storage, and your locations; and set Screen Time limits for your children.

Share purchases and storage with Family Sharing. Up to six members of your family can share their purchases from the App Store, Apple TV app, Apple Books, and iTunes Store and share the same storage plan—even if they each use their own iCloud account. Pay for family purchases with one credit card, and approve your kids' spending right from your MacBook Pro, iOS device, or iPadOS device. Share locations, so you can help family members find lost devices.

Account Recovery. Add one or more people you trust as a recovery contact or set up a recovery key to help you reset your password and regain access to your account.

40

Apple ID

Apple ID: ashley_rico1@icloud.com

Password: Change Password...
Last Changed October 18, 2021.

Two-Factor Authentication: ● On
Your trusted devices and phone numbers are used to verify your identity when signing in.

Trusted phone numbers: 1   Edit...
Trusted phone numbers are used to verify your identity when signing in on a different device or browser.

Get a verification code to sign in on another device or at iCloud.com.

Get Verification Code

Account Recovery   Manage...
Your account recovery information can help you get back into your account if you get locked out. Learn More...

Ashley Rico
ashley_rico1@icloud.com

Overview
Name, Phone, Email
Password & Security
Payment & Shipping

iCloud
Media & Purchases
Not Signed In

Ashley's MacBook...
This MacBook Pro

Find your way around

The desktop, menu bar, and Help on your Mac

The first thing you see on your MacBook Pro is the desktop, where you can quickly open apps, search for anything on your MacBook Pro and the web, organize your files, and more.

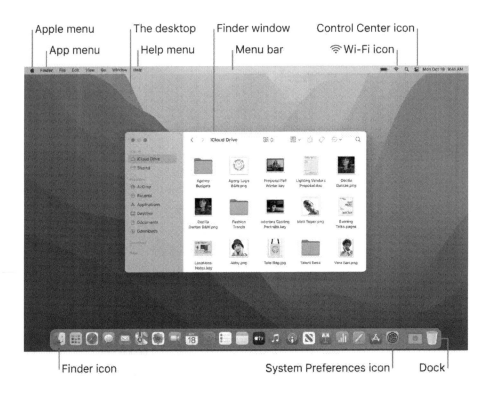

Apple menu | The desktop | Finder window | Control Center icon
App menu | Help menu | Menu bar | Wi-Fi icon

Finder icon | System Preferences icon | Dock

Tip: Can't find the pointer on the screen? To magnify it temporarily, move your finger rapidly back and forth on the trackpad. Or if you're using a mouse, slide it back and forth quickly.

Menu bar. The menu bar runs along the top of the screen. Use the menus on the left side to choose commands and perform tasks in apps. The menu items change, depending on which app you're using. Use the icons on the right side to connect to a Wi-Fi network, check your Wi-Fi status , open Control Center , check your battery charge , search using Spotlight , and more.

Tip: You can change the icons that appear in the menu bar.

Apple menu . The Apple menu contains frequently used items and always appears in the upper-left corner of the screen. To open it, click the Apple icon .

42

App menu. You can have multiple apps and windows open at the same time. The name of the app that's active appears in bold to the right of the Apple menu , followed by that app's unique menus. If you open a different app or click an open window in a different app, the name of the app menu changes to that app and the menus in the menu bar change along with it. If you're looking for a command in a menu and can't find it, check the app menu to see if the app you want is active.

Help menu. Help for your MacBook Pro is always available in the menu bar. To get help, open the Finder in the Dock, click the Help menu, and choose macOS Help to open the macOS User Guide. Or type in the search field and choose a suggestion. To get help for a specific app, open the app and click Help in the menu bar.

Stay organized with stacks. You can gather files on the desktop into stacks to keep them organized in groups (by kind, date, or tag), and to keep your desktop orderly. To view what's inside a stack, click the stack to expand its contents, or place your pointer over a stack to view thumbnail images of the files. To create stacks on your desktop, click the desktop, then choose View > Use Stacks. To see grouping options for your stacks, go to View > Group Stacks By and choose an option. Then any new files you add to the desktop are automatically sorted into the appropriate stack.

The Finder on your Mac

Represented by the blue icon with the smiling face, the Finder is the home base for your Mac. You use it to organize and access almost everything on your Mac, including documents, images, movies, and any other files you have. To open a Finder window, click the Finder icon in the Dock at the bottom of the screen. Force click a file icon to quickly view its contents, or force click a filename to edit it.

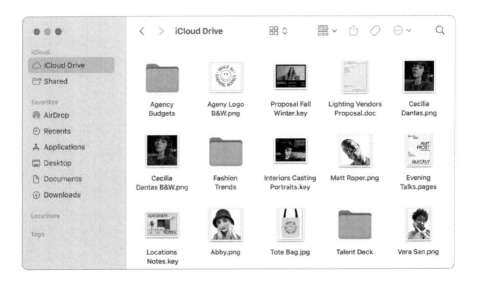

The Finder window. Click the pop-up menu button at the top of the Finder window to change how you view documents and folders. View them as icons, in a list, in hierarchical columns, or in a gallery. The sidebar on the left shows icons for the items you use often or want to open quickly. To see all your documents stored on iCloud Drive, click the iCloud Drive folder in the sidebar, and to see only the documents you're sharing and that are shared with you, click the Shared folder. To change what's shown in the sidebar, choose Finder > Preferences.

Get organized. Your Mac has folders already created for common types of content—Documents, Pictures, Applications, Music, and more. As you create documents, install apps, and do other work, you can create new folders to stay organized. To create a new folder, choose File > New Folder.

Sync devices. When you connect a device like an iPhone or iPad, it appears in the Finder sidebar. Double-click the device's icon to see options to back up, update, sync, and restore your device.

Gallery View. With Gallery View, you can see a large preview of your selected file, so you can visually identify your images, video clips, and other documents. The Preview pane on the right shows information to help you identify the file you want. Use the scrubber bar at the bottom to quickly locate what you're looking for. To close or open the Preview pane, press Shift-Command-P. To show the Preview pane options in the Finder, choose View > Show Preview. To customize what's shown, choose View > Show Preview Options, then select the options for your file type.

Tip: To show filenames in Gallery View, press Command-J and select "Show filename."

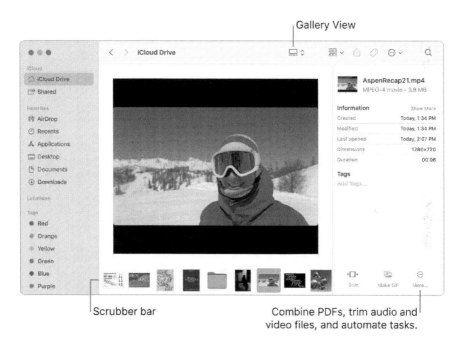

Gallery View

Scrubber bar

Combine PDFs, trim audio and video files, and automate tasks.

Quick Actions. In Gallery View, click the More button at the bottom right of the Finder window for shortcuts to manage and edit files directly in the Finder. You can rotate an image, annotate or crop an image in Markup, combine images and PDFs into a single file, trim audio and video files, run shortcuts created with the Shortcuts app, and create custom actions through Automator workflows (for example, watermarking a file).

Quick Look. Select a file and press the Space bar to open Quick Look. Use the buttons at the top of the Quick Look window to sign PDFs; trim audio and video files; and mark up, rotate, and crop images without opening a separate app.

Tip: You can add alternative image descriptions that can be read by VoiceOver using Markup in Preview or Quick Look.

Get there faster. The Go menu in the menu bar is a quick way to get to folders and locations. Instead of using several clicks to navigate to the Utilities folder, choose Go > Utilities. You can also choose Go > Enclosing Folder to return to the top level of nested folders. If you know the path to a specific folder, choose Go > Go to Folder, then type the path.

13-inch MacBook Pro: Use the Finder with the Touch Bar

Use the Finder with the Touch Bar on your 13-inch MacBook Pro

Use the Touch Bar, at the top of your keyboard, to perform Finder tasks and more.

Use the Touch Bar. Tap buttons to move back and forth through items you've viewed, set view options, and quickly look at, share, or tag an item.

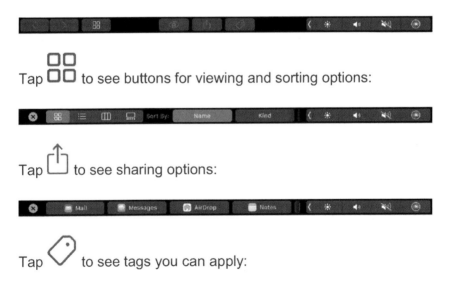

Tap ⬚⬚ to see buttons for viewing and sorting options:

Tap ⬆ to see sharing options:

Tap ◇ to see tags you can apply:

The Dock on your Mac

The Dock, at the bottom of the screen, is a convenient place to keep the apps and documents you use frequently.

Go to the Finder.   Open System Preferences.

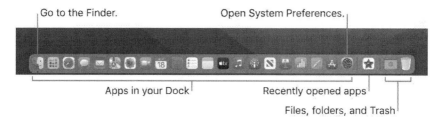

Apps in your Dock   Recently opened apps

Files, folders, and Trash

Open an app or file. Click an app icon in the Dock, or click the Launchpad icon ▦ in the Dock to see all the apps on your Mac, then click the app you want. You can also search for an app using Spotlight ⌕ (in the top-right corner of the menu bar), then open the app directly from your Spotlight search results. Recently opened apps appear in the center section of the Dock.

Close an app. When you click the red dot in the top-left corner of an open window, the window closes but the app stays open. Open apps have a black dot beneath them in the Dock. To close an app, choose "Quit appname" from the app menu (for example, in the Mail app, choose Quit Mail from the Mail menu). Or Control-click the app icon in the Dock and click Quit.

Indicates an open app

Add an item to the Dock. Drag the item and drop it where you want it. Place apps in the left section of the Dock, and files or folders in the right section.

Remove an item from the Dock. Drag it out of the Dock. The item isn't removed from your MacBook Pro—just from the Dock.

See everything that's open on your Mac. Press the Mission

Control key 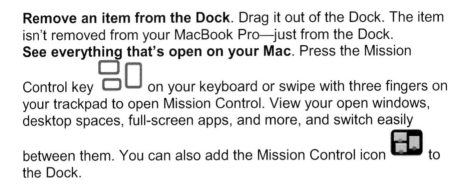 on your keyboard or swipe with three fingers on your trackpad to open Mission Control. View your open windows, desktop spaces, full-screen apps, and more, and switch easily

between them. You can also add the Mission Control icon ![icon] to the Dock.

See all open windows in an app. Force click an app in the Dock to view all the app's open windows.

Tip: Click Dock & Menu Bar in System Preferences to change the appearance and behavior of the Dock. Make the Dock larger or smaller, move it to the left or right side of the screen, set it to hide when you're not using it, and more.

Notification Center on your Mac

Notification Center keeps all of your important information, reminders, and widgets in one convenient place. Get details about calendar events, stocks, weather, and more—and catch up on notifications you might have missed (emails, messages, reminders, and more).

Open Notification Center. Click the date or time at the top right of the screen, or swipe left from the right edge of the trackpad with two fingers. Scroll down to see more.

Click to open Notification Center.

Focus on what you're doing. When you're working, having dinner, or just don't want to be disturbed, Focus can automatically filter your notifications so you see only the ones you specify. Focus can pause all notifications or allow only certain ones to appear, and sends an auto-reply—called a Focus Status—to people trying to reach you, so they know your notifications are silenced. You can set or customize a Focus to fit what you're currently doing, and allow notifications from certain people or apps, for phone calls or upcoming events, and more. To set up Focus, open System Preferences , click Notifications & Focus, then click Focus. To turn Focus on or off, click in the menu bar, then click the Focus section and choose a Focus.

Interact with your notifications. Reply to an email, listen to the latest podcast, or view details about calendar events. Click the arrow in the top-right corner of a notification to view options, take action, or get more information.

Customize your widgets. Click Edit Widgets (at the bottom of your notifications) to add, remove, or rearrange widgets. You can also add third-party widgets from the Mac App Store.
Set your notification preferences. Open System Preferences, click Notifications & Focus, then click Notifications to select which notifications you see. Notifications are sorted by most recent, and redesigned Today widgets deliver information at a glance.

Control Center groups all your menu bar extras into a single place, giving you instant access to the controls you use the most—like Bluetooth, AirDrop, Mic Mode, Screen Mirroring, Focus, and brightness and volume controls—right from the menu bar. Click in the upper-right corner of the screen to open Control Center.

Monitor your mic. The recording indicator shows when your computer's microphone is in use or if it was used recently. This light increases security and privacy on your Mac by letting you know if an app has access to the microphone.

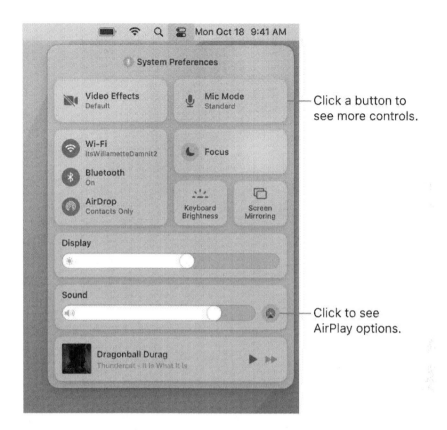

Click a button to see more controls.

Click to see AirPlay options.

Click for more options. Click a button to see more options. For example, click the Wi-Fi button to see your preferred networks, other networks, or to open Network Preferences. To return to the main Control Center view, click again.

Pin your Control Center favorites. Drag a favorite item from Control Center to the menu bar to pin it there, so you can easily access it with a single click. To change what appears in Control Center and in the menu bar, open Dock & Menu Bar preferences, select a control on the left, then click "Show in Menu Bar" or "Show in Control Center." You see a preview of where the control will appear in the menu bar. Some items can't be added to or removed from Control Center or the menu bar.

Tip: To quickly remove an item from the menu bar, press and hold the Command key and drag the item out of the menu bar.

Click a feature to view where it appears.

Select "Show in Menu Bar" to see a feature's location in the menu bar.

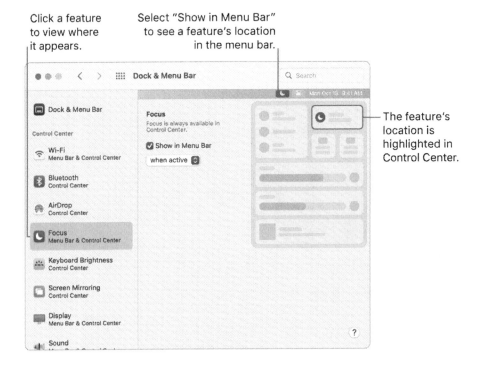

The feature's location is highlighted in Control Center.

System Preferences on your Mac

System Preferences is the place where you personalize your MacBook Pro settings. For example, use Battery preferences to change sleep settings. Or use Desktop & Screen Saver preferences to add a desktop picture or choose a screen saver.

Customize your MacBook Pro. Click the System Preferences icon in the Dock, or choose Apple menu > System Preferences. Then click the type of preference you want to set.

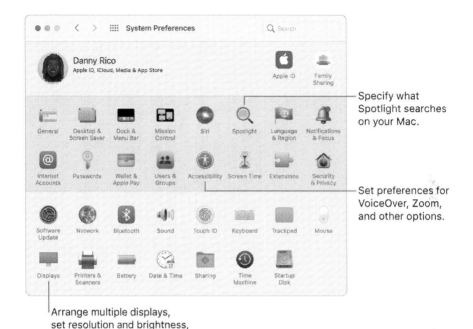

Specify what Spotlight searches on your Mac.

Set preferences for VoiceOver, Zoom, and other options.

Arrange multiple displays, set resolution and brightness, and more.

Update macOS. In System Preferences, click Software Update to see if your Mac is running the latest version of macOS software. You can specify options for automatic software updates.

Spotlight on your Mac

Spotlight is an easy way to find anything on your MacBook Pro, such as documents, contacts, calendar events, and email messages. Spotlight Suggestions offer info from Wikipedia articles, web search results, news, sports, weather, stocks, movies, and other sources.

Search for anything. Click at the top right of the screen, then start typing.

Tip: Type Command–Space bar to show or hide the Spotlight search field.

Start typing, and results
appear quickly.

Convert currencies and measurements. Enter a currency—like $,
€, or ¥—and an amount, then press Return to get a list of converted
values. Or specify a unit of measure for measurement conversions.

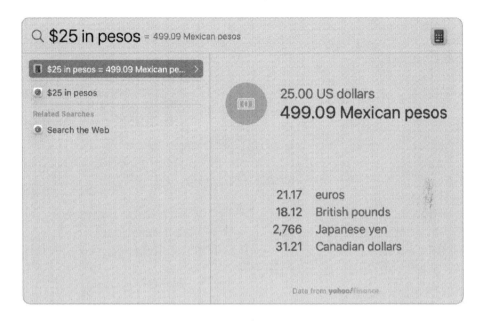

Open an app. Enter the app name in Spotlight, then press Return.

Turn off Spotlight Suggestions. If you want Spotlight to search only for items on your MacBook Pro, open System Preferences, click Spotlight, then click to deselect Siri Suggestions. You can also make other changes to the list of categories Spotlight searches.

Siri on your Mac

You can activate Siri with your voice on your MacBook Pro and use Siri for many tasks. For example, you can schedule meetings, change preferences, get answers, send messages, place calls, and add items to your calendar. Use Siri to give you directions ("How do I get home from here?"), provide information ("How high is Mount Whitney?"), perform basic tasks ("Create a new grocery list"), and much more.

If you enable the "Listen for 'Hey Siri'" option in Siri preferences, Siri is available whenever you say "Hey Siri" and immediately speak your request.

Note: To use Siri, your Mac must be connected to the internet. Siri may not be available in all languages or in all areas, and features may vary by area.

Enable and activate Siri. Open System Preferences, click Siri, and set options. If you enabled Siri during setup, on the 13-inch MacBook Pro, tap the Siri button in the Control Strip on the Touch Bar or press and hold Command-Space bar to open Siri. On the 14-inch or 16-inch MacBook Pro, press and hold the Dictation/Siri (F5) key to open Siri. Or click Siri in System Preferences, then select Enable Ask Siri. You can set other preferences in the Siri pane, such as the language and voice to use and whether to show Siri in the menu bar.

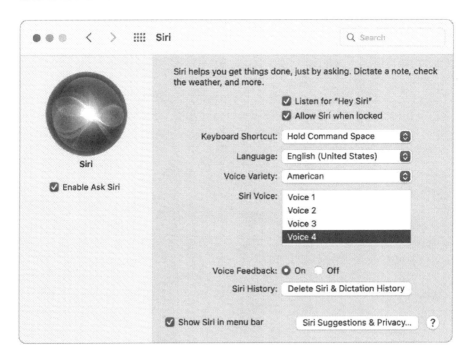

Tip: You can add the Siri icon to the menu bar by selecting that option in the Siri pane of **System Preferences**. Then click the Siri icon to use Siri.

Hey Siri. On your MacBook Pro, you can simply say "Hey Siri" to get responses to your requests. To enable this feature in the Siri pane of System Preferences, click "Listen for 'Hey Siri'," then speak several Siri commands when prompted.

For convenience, "Hey Siri" doesn't respond when the lid to your MacBook Pro is closed. If the lid is closed and connected to an external display, you can still activate Siri from the icon in the menu bar.

Play some music. Just say "Play some music," and Siri does the rest. You can even tell Siri, "Play the top song from March 1991."

Drag and drop. Drag and drop images and locations from the Siri window into an email, text message, or document. You can also copy and paste text.

Change the voice. Click Siri in System Preferences, then choose an option from the Siri Voice menu.

Throughout this guide, you'll find suggestions for things you can use Siri for—they look like this:

Ask Siri. Say something like:
- "Open the Keynote presentation I was working on last night"
- "What time is it in Paris?"

Window management on your Mac

It's easy to find yourself with a dozen open apps and one or more windows for each app open on your desktop. Luckily, there are some efficient ways to see and navigate the windows you have open. When you want to focus, you can expand one app to fill the whole screen or choose two apps to share the screen. When you need to find a window that's buried, use Mission Control to show all your open windows in a single layer. You can even create multiple desktops (called spaces) to view only specific windows, and then move between the spaces.

Click to see
window options.

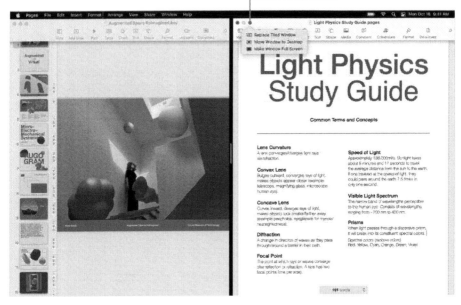

Use the whole screen. Use full-screen view when you want your app to fill the whole screen. Many apps on your Mac, such as Keynote, Numbers, and Pages, support full-screen view. In full screen, the menu bar is hidden until you move the pointer over the top of the screen, or you can choose to always show the menu bar. To enter or leave full-screen view, move the pointer over the green button in the top-left corner of the window, then choose Enter Full Screen from the menu that appears.

Split the screen. Use Split View to work in two app windows side by side. Like full screen, the two windows fill the screen. Move the pointer to the green button in the top-left corner of a window you want to use, then choose Tile Window to Left of Screen or Tile Window to Right of Screen from the menu that appears. Click another window and it automatically fills the other half of the screen. When the pointer is over the green button, the menu that appears has options to switch apps, take the two windows to full screen, and more.

Mission Control. Quickly move your open windows into a single layer, then click a window to return to regular view with that window in front and active. If you have additional desktops (spaces) or have apps in Split View, they appear in a row along the top of the screen.

To enter or leave Mission Control, press 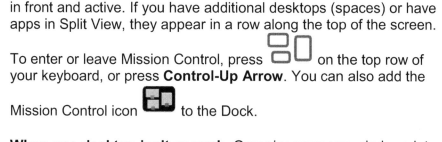 on the top row of your keyboard, or press **Control-Up Arrow**. You can also add the Mission Control icon to the Dock.

When one desktop isn't enough. Organize your app windows into multiple desktop spaces, then switch between them as you work. To create a space, enter Mission Control and click the Add Desktop button . Use keyboard shortcuts and Mission Control to move between your spaces. You can drag windows from one space to another and add or delete spaces as you work.

That horizontal traffic light. The red, yellow, and green buttons in the top-left corner of every window aren't just for show. Click the red button to close an app window. For some apps, this quits the app and closes all open windows for the app. For others, it closes the current window but leaves the app open. The yellow button closes the window temporarily and puts it in the right side of the Dock. When you want to reopen it, click it in the Dock to expand it. And the green button is a quick way to change your windows to full screen and Split View, and more.

Display settings for your Mac

Match the light in your surroundings. Your MacBook Pro has a Retina display with True Tone® technology. True Tone automatically adapts the color of the display to match the light in your environment for a more natural viewing experience. Turn True Tone on or off in the Displays pane of System Preferences.

Use a dynamic desktop. When you use a dynamic desktop picture, the desktop picture automatically changes to match the time of day in your location. Click Desktop & Screen Saver in System Preferences, click Desktop, then choose a picture for Dynamic Desktop. To have your screen change based on your time zone, enable Location Services. If Location Services is turned off, the picture changes based on the time zone specified in Date & Time preferences.

Stay focused with Dark Mode. You can use a dark color scheme for the desktop, menu bar, Dock, and all the built-in macOS apps. Your content stands out front and center while darkened controls and windows recede into the background. See white text on a black background in apps such as Mail, Contacts, Calendar, and Messages, so it's easier on your eyes when you're working in dark environments.

Dark Mode is finely tuned for professionals who edit photos and images—colors and fine details pop against the dark app backgrounds. But it's also great for anyone who just wants to focus on their content.

Night Shift. Switch your Mac to warmer colors at night or in low-light conditions to reduce your exposure to bright blue light. Blue light can make it harder to fall asleep, so warmer screen colors may help you get a better night's rest. You can schedule Night Shift to turn on and off automatically at specific times, or set it to come on from sunset to sunrise. In System Preferences, click Displays, click the Night Shift button at the bottom, then set your options. Drag the slider to adjust the color temperature.

Connect a display. You can connect an external display, a projector, or an HDTV to your Mac.

Transfer your data to your new MacBook Pro

It's easy to copy your files and settings wirelessly from another Mac or PC to your MacBook Pro. You can transfer information to your MacBook Pro from an existing computer or from a Time Machine backup on a USB storage device.

You might need to upgrade the macOS version on your older computer before you can transfer the information on it—Migration Assistant requires macOS 10.7 or later, but it's best to update your older computer to the latest version possible.

Tip: For best results, make sure your new MacBook Pro is running the latest version of macOS. Open System Preferences, then click Software Update to check for updates.

Transfer wirelessly. If you didn't transfer your data when you first set up your MacBook Pro, you can use Migration Assistant at any time. Open a Finder window, go to Applications, open the Utilities folder, then double-click Migration Assistant and follow the onscreen instructions. Make sure both computers are connected to the same network, and keep the computers near each other throughout the migration process.

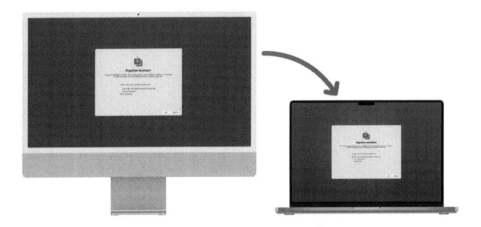

Tip: To transfer the information wirelessly from your existing computer to your MacBook Pro, make sure both computers are connected to the same network. Keep both computers near each other throughout the migration process.

If you used Time Machine to back up your files from another Mac to a storage device (such as an external disk), you can copy the files from the device to your MacBook Pro.

Copy files from a storage device. Connect the storage device to your MacBook Pro using an appropriate adapter if necessary. Then drag files from the storage device to your MacBook Pro.

Back up and restore your Mac

To keep your files safe, it's important to back up your MacBook Pro regularly. The easiest way to back up is to use Time Machine—which is built into your Mac—to back up your apps, accounts, preferences, music, photos, movies, and documents (it doesn't back up the macOS operating system). Use Time Machine to back up to an external storage device connected to your MacBook Pro, or to a supported network volume.

Tip: You can use a shared Mac that's on the same network as your MacBook Pro as a backup destination. On the other Mac, go to the Sharing pane of System Preferences, then turn on File Sharing. Add a shared folder, Control-click the folder, choose Advanced Options, then click "Share as Time Machine backup destination."

Set up Time Machine. Make sure your MacBook Pro is on the same Wi-Fi network as your external storage device, or connect the external storage device to your MacBook Pro. Open System Preferences, click Time Machine, then select Back Up Automatically. Select the drive you want to use for backup, and you're all set.

Accessibility on your Mac

Your Mac, iOS devices, and iPadOS devices include powerful tools to make Apple product features available and easy to use by all. There are four main accessibility focus areas for your Mac. Click a link to learn more about the features for each area:
- Vision
- Hearing
- Mobility
- Cognitive

Accessibility preferences. In System Preferences, Accessibility preferences are organized around topics of vision, hearing, and motor, making it simpler to find what you're looking for.
Do it all with Voice Control. You can control your Mac with just your voice. All audio processing for Voice Control happens on your Mac, so your personal data is kept private.
Accurate dictation. If you can't type by hand, accurate dictation is essential for communication. Voice Control brings the latest advances in machine learning for speech-to-text transcription.

You can add custom words to help Voice Control recognize the words you commonly use. Choose System Preferences > Accessibility, select Voice Control, then click Vocabulary and add the words you want. To customize commands in the Voice Control preferences page, click Commands, then select to keep default commands, or add new ones.

Note: The dictation accuracy improvements are for these languages: English (US, UK, India, Australia), Mandarin Chinese (China mainland), Cantonese (Hong Kong), Japanese (Japan), Spanish (Mexico, Latin America, Spain), French (France), and German (Germany).

Rich text editing. Rich text editing commands in Voice Control let you quickly make corrections and move on to expressing your next idea. You can replace one phrase with another, quickly position the pointer to make edits, and select text with precision. Try saying "Replace 'John will be there soon' with 'John just arrived'." When you correct words, word and emoji suggestions help you quickly select what you want.

Comprehensive navigation. Use voice commands to open and interact with apps. To click an item, just say its accessibility label name. You can also say "show numbers" to see number labels appear next to all clickable items, and then say a number to click. If you need to touch a part of the screen without a control, you can say "show grid" to superimpose a grid on your screen and do things like click, zoom, drag, and more.

Hover and zoom. Use Hover Text to display high-resolution text for screen items under your pointer. Press Command while hovering over text with the pointer, and a window with zoomed text appears on your screen.

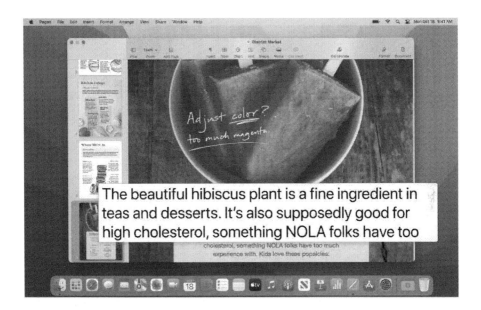

The beautiful hibiscus plant is a fine ingredient in teas and desserts. It's also supposedly good for high cholesterol, something NOLA folks have too

Zoom Display lets you keep one monitor zoomed in tightly and another at its standard resolution. View the same screen up close and at a distance simultaneously.

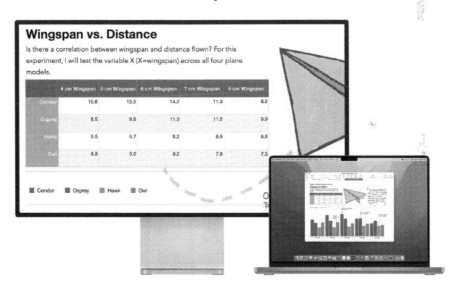

Make an easy-to-see custom pointer. Customize the outline and fill color of the mouse pointer so it's easier to recognize when it

moves or changes to an insertion point, crosshair, hand, or other shape.

Improved keyboard access. An expanded set of keyboard shortcuts allows you to control everything on your Mac with a keyboard—no mouse or trackpad required.

Use VoiceOver, the built-in screen reader. VoiceOver describes aloud what appears on the screen and speaks the text in documents, webpages, and windows. Using VoiceOver, you control your Mac with the keyboard or trackpad gestures, or connect a refreshable braille display to use with VoiceOver. To customize VoiceOver, use VoiceOver Utility.
Ask Siri. Say something like:
- "Turn VoiceOver on."
- "Turn VoiceOver off."

Use Siri for VoiceOver. If you prefer the natural voice of Siri, you can choose to use Siri for VoiceOver or Speech. Simplified keyboard navigation requires less drilling into unique focus groups—making it even easier to navigate with VoiceOver. You can also store custom punctuation marks in iCloud, and choose from International Braille tables. And if you're a developer, VoiceOver now reads aloud line numbers, break points, warnings, and errors in the Xcode text editor.
VoiceOver image descriptions. Using Markup in Preview or Quick Look, you can add alternative image descriptions that can be read by VoiceOver. Image descriptions persist even when shared and can be read by a range of supported apps on iPhone, iPad, and Mac.
VoiceOver PDF signature descriptions. Add custom descriptions to your PDF signatures so you can identify them quickly and choose the right one.

Color enhancements. If you have a color vision deficiency, you can adjust your Mac display colors using color filter options. It's easy to turn this preference on or off to quickly differentiate a color using the Accessibility Options panel, which you can access by triple-pressing Touch ID.

Customize your Memoji. macOS Monterey introduces new customizations for Memoji, including cochlear implants, oxygen tubes, and a soft helmet for headwear.

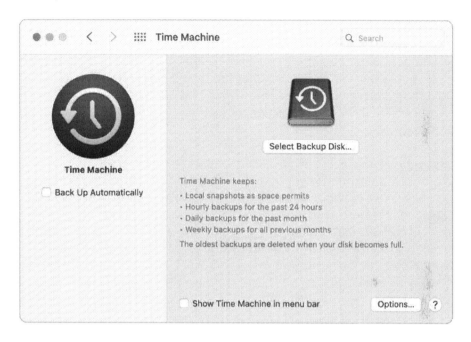

Back up with iCloud. Files in iCloud Drive and photos in iCloud Photos are automatically stored in iCloud and don't need to be part of your Time Machine backup. However, if you'd like to back them up, do the following:

- **iCloud Drive**: Open System Preferences, click Apple ID, then click iCloud and deselect Optimize Mac Storage. The contents of your iCloud Drive will be stored on your Mac and included in your backup.
- **iCloud Photos**: Open Photos, then choose Photos > Preferences. In the iCloud pane, select "Download Originals to this Mac." Full-resolution versions of your entire photo library will be stored on your Mac and included in your backup.

Restore your files. You can use Time Machine to restore all your files at once. Click the Time Machine icon in the menu bar, then choose Enter Time Machine. (If the Time Machine icon isn't in the menu bar, choose Apple Menu > System Preferences, click Time Machine, then select "Show Time Machine in menu bar.") Select one or more items that you want to restore (individual folders or your entire disk), then click Restore.

If you use Time Machine to back up your Mac, you can recover your files if the operating system or startup disk is damaged. To do this, you must first reinstall macOS on your Mac before you can restore your files using your Time Machine backup. Read on for more information.

Reinstall macOS. Your operating system files are kept separate from your personal files in a sealed system disk. However, some actions, like erasing or inadvertently damaging a disk, require that you restore your MacBook Pro. You can reinstall macOS and then use Time Machine to restore your personal files from your backup. With macOS Big Sur and later, there are several ways to restore your Mac. You may be required to install a newer version of macOS than what your computer originally came with, or what you were using before the disk was damaged.

Important: Advanced users may want to create a bootable installer to reinstall macOS in the future. This can be useful if you want to use a specific version of macOS.

Restore factory settings. You can restore your Mac to its original state by erasing your Mac, then using macOS Recovery to reinstall macOS.

New features on your MacBook Pro

macOS Monterey introduces tools to bring you closer with family, colleagues, and friends, and work more fluidly across all your devices.

The new communication and connection features of macOS Monterey include:

- **FaceTime**: Create a link to set up a FaceTime call for later, share with a group, or add to a Calendar event. A new Grid View makes it easy to see who's speaking. You can even use a link to invite people on non-Apple devices to join a call using FaceTime on the web. With new Voice Isolation and Wide Spectrum modes, your mic captures only the sounds you want. Keep the focus on you and blur your background with Portrait mode (available on your Mac with Apple silicon).
- **Messages**: View multiple photos in collages or stacks that you can flip through. Pin important content so it gets priority in searches, Shared with You, and conversation details.
- **Shared with You**: Content you receive in Messages automatically appears in a new Shared with You section in the corresponding app, so you can enjoy it whenever it's convenient. Content only appears in Shared with You if the

friend who sent it is in your Contacts. Shared with You is featured in the Photos, Safari, News, Podcasts, and TV apps.

- **AirPlay to Mac**: Now you can watch videos, listen to music, and more on your Mac as they're being played on your other devices.

Here are improvements to increase your productivity:

- **Safari**: Safari reimagines the browser, providing a more immersive and personal experience across your devices. Get more space to browse websites, with the new unified tab bar. Easily switch between investigating your next big trip, exploring gift options, and doing essential research with Tab Groups. The new tab bar, extensions, and start page are now available across Mac, iPhone, and iPad, so you get the same Safari everywhere you browse. Other features include improved Intelligent Tracking Prevention and Hide My Email.
- **Focus and Notification Center**: When you're working, having dinner, or just don't want to be disturbed, Focus can automatically filter your notifications so you see only the ones you want.
- **Quick Note and Notes**: Notes now supports tags (for example, #research)—to help you organize and search your notes—and mentions (@username), so that you can alert collaborators to changes in a shared note. A new Activity view displays a summary of updates since you last viewed a shared note. With Quick Note, you can create a note anywhere on your Mac—in an app or webpage, or even on the desktop.

Check out these intelligence and automation features:

- **Photos, Visual Look Up, and Live Text**: There's newly improved people identification and naming, new features for editing and playing back Memories, and the ability to import photos from a second Photos library. Quickly see photos shared with you in Messages, and respond in Photos. Learn about objects in the photo in Visual Look Up and interact with text using Live Text.

- **Shortcuts**: Quickly perform tasks using one or more apps or actions. Create your own shortcuts, or choose from a curated list of shortcuts available in the Gallery and keep your shortcuts synced across all your devices. Run shortcuts with your voice, from the Dock, Menu Bar, Finder, and more.

macOS Monterey also provides these new features and enhancements to existing features to improve your productivity and creativity:

- **Maps**: A new design helps you find what you're looking for and get there sooner. Explore natural features with an interactive 3D globe and discover new city experiences with landmarks, elevation, and more, available on your Mac with Apple silicon. You can filter to see what's open now and save your favorite places and transit lines for later. Nearby transit information and new driving maps will help you plan where you're going and get there quicker.
- **Apple ID**: Add your Memoji to your Apple account. Set up a contact and PIN to help you recover your account if you get locked out.
- **iCloud+**: This premium subscription service gives you more iCloud storage for your photos and files, plus additional features such as Private Relay (beta), Hide My Email, and HomeKit Secure Video support. iCloud+ availability varies by country or region.
- **Accessibility**: Updates to VoiceOver include the ability to add image descriptions with Markup, PDF signature descriptions, improved keyboard access, custom mouse pointers, and new accessibility Memoji to better reflect your appearance.
- **App Store and Games**: The new multiplayer friend selector makes it easy to invite your recent Messages friends and groups to play Game Center-enabled games. Games you download from the App Store now appear automatically in the new Games folder in Launchpad, so they're always easy to access, even with a game controller.
- **Books**: Explore new features like Reading Goals, Want to Read, and Reading Now, previously available only on iOS. Find books quicker with search results that come up as soon as you start typing. Enjoy personalized recommendations for

books, audiobooks, and genre collections in your search results and buy directly from the Search tab.

- **Finder improvements**: An enhanced "go to folder" window features a new look and improved autocompletion engine to help you get to the files or folder you're looking for more quickly. Run shortcuts from the menu bar and the Quick Actions menu. A new collaboration folder in the sidebar contains all shared documents, and displays sharing-related metadata. As you move windows from your Mac to a secondary display, the windows resize to fit the new display.
- **Find My**: Share your location with family and friends. With Separation Alerts, get notified on your iPhone, iPad, or iPod touch if you leave your Mac with Apple silicon behind.
- **Hello screen saver and desktop picture**: The Hello screen saver writes "hello" on the screen in 34 languages using fresh animation and a font inspired by the original Mac. You can also use a Hello desktop picture available in several colors with light, dark, or dynamic options. Set these in the

  Desktop & Screen Saver pane of System Preferences .
- **Passwords**: Look up and manage your saved passwords for apps and websites in the new Passwords pane in System Preferences. Import passwords from other password managers, then use AutoFill when signing in to apps and websites.
- **Reminders**: Use tags and Custom Smart Lists to organize and filter reminders. Other improvements include reminder deletion, enhanced natural language, and expanded suggestions.
- **Split View/Window Management**: Manage multiple open windows efficiently with new options for Split View and full-screen view. In Split View, click the green button in the top-left corner of a window to swap apps or go to full screen (both apps in Split View go to full screen). And in full-screen view, you can keep the menu bar visible if you prefer.
- **Translation**: Translate text in Safari, Mail, Pages, Preview, and other apps. You can replace selected text with the translation, switch between languages, and more. With Live Text, you can even translate selected text in photos. Translation is available system-wide and in some third-party apps. Not all languages are available.

Use MacBook Pro with other devices

Use your MacBook Pro with iCloud and Continuity

With iCloud, you can keep your information up to date on all your devices and collaborate with friends and family. Your MacBook Pro works seamlessly with your iPhone, iPad, iPod touch, or Apple Watch when you use iCloud and sign in to each of them with the same Apple ID. You can transfer files, share and edit documents, unlock your MacBook Pro with your Apple Watch, turn your iPhone or iPad into an internet hotspot, answer calls or send texts from your MacBook Pro, and more.

If you didn't turn on iCloud when you first set up your Mac, open System Preferences, click Sign In, then sign in with your Apple ID, or create a new Apple ID if you don't have one. Click iCloud, then turn iCloud features on or off.

Access your content across devices. With iCloud, you can securely store, edit, and share your documents, photos, and videos across devices to make sure you're always up to date.

Use your MacBook Pro with other devices. Seamlessly move content between your MacBook Pro and other devices using Continuity. Just sign in on each device with your Apple ID, and whenever your MacBook Pro and devices are near each other, they work together in convenient ways. You can start a task on one device and finish it on another, copy and paste between devices, answer calls or send texts from your MacBook Pro, transfer files with AirDrop, and more.

Access your iCloud content on your Mac

iCloud helps you keep your most important information—like your photos, files, and more—safe, up to date, and available across all your devices. It's built into every Apple device, and everyone gets 5 GB of storage to start. Purchases you make from the App Store, Apple TV app, Apple Books, or iTunes Store don't count toward your available space. So if you have an iPhone, iPad, or iPod touch, just sign in on each device with your Apple ID, turn on iCloud, and you'll have everything you need. You can upgrade to iCloud+ if you need more storage and premium features including iCloud Private Relay (beta), Hide My Email, Custom email domains, and HomeKit Secure Video support.

Automatically store your desktop and Documents folder in iCloud Drive. You can save files in your Documents folder or on your desktop, and they're automatically available on iCloud Drive and accessible wherever you are. When working with iCloud Drive, you have access to files on your MacBook Pro, on your iPhone or iPad in the Files app, on the web at iCloud.com, or on a Windows PC in the iCloud for Windows app. When you make changes to a file on a device or on iCloud Drive, you'll see your edits wherever you view the file.

To get started, open System Preferences, click Apple ID, then click iCloud. Select iCloud Drive, then click Options and select "Desktop & Documents Folders.".

Store and share photos with iCloud Photos and Shared Albums. Store your photo library in iCloud and see your photos and videos, as well as the edits you make to them, on all your devices. Share photos and videos with only the people you choose, and let them add their own photos, videos, and comments. To get started, open System Preferences, click Apple ID, click iCloud, then select Photos.

Enjoy your purchases anywhere. When you're signed in to your devices with the same Apple ID, purchases you've made on the App Store, Apple TV app, Apple Books, and iTunes Store are available at any time, no matter which computer or device you used to purchase them. So all your music, movies, books, and more are available wherever you go.

Locate your MacBook Pro with Find My Mac. If your MacBook Pro is missing, you can use Find My to locate it on a map, lock its screen, and even erase its data remotely if you have Find My Mac turned on. To turn on Find My Mac, open System Preferences, click Apple ID, click iCloud, then select Find My Mac.

Note: If your MacBook Pro has multiple user accounts, only one can have Find My Mac turned on.

Do more with iCloud+. iCloud+ is a subscription service that gives you all the storage tiers and sharing features of iCloud but with additional features. You can share any size iCloud+ storage plan through Family Sharing. iCloud+ also includes iCloud Private Relay (beta), HomeKit Secure Video, and custom email domains for your Mail address on iCloud.com. Here's what you get with an iCloud+ subscription:

- **Storage**: 50 GB, 200 GB, or 2 TB of iCloud storage.
- **iCloud Private Relay (beta)**: Private Relay is an internet privacy service that hides your IP address in Safari and protects your unencrypted traffic. When it's on, you can browse the web with extra security and privacy.
- **Hide My Email**: Create unique, random email addresses that forward to your personal inbox, so you can send and receive email without having to share your personal email address.
- **HomeKit Secure Video**: Connect your home security cameras in the Home App to record your footage and view it from anywhere. It's all end-to-end encrypted, and none of the video counts against your iCloud storage.
- **Custom email domains**: Personalize your iCloud Mail address with a custom domain name. You can invite your family members to use the same domain with their iCloud Mail accounts.
- **Family Sharing**: All iCloud+ plans can be shared with up to five family members, so everyone can enjoy all these features and included storage with a single subscription.

Screen Time on Mac

Screen Time shows you how you spend time in apps and on websites. It also lets you monitor what your kids are doing on their Apple devices.

Set your limits. Set limits to control how much time you spend with specific apps, categories of apps, and websites. You can also view reports to see how much time you're spending with apps and websites, and schedule downtime away from your Mac.

Family sharing. Parents can configure Screen Time on their Mac— or iPhone or iPad—and everything is set up for their kids on their devices.

One-tap media ratings. While setting up Screen Time for your kids, you can set age-based media ratings for the Music and Books apps.

Use Handoff on your Mac

With Handoff, you can continue on one device where you left off on another. Work on a presentation on your MacBook Pro, then continue on your iPad. Or start an email message on your iPhone, then finish it on your MacBook Pro. View a message on your Apple Watch, and respond to it on your MacBook Pro. You don't have to worry about transferring files. When your MacBook Pro and devices are near each other, an icon appears in the Dock whenever an activity can be handed off; to continue, just click the icon.

Note: To use Handoff, you need an iPhone or iPod touch with iOS 8 or later, or an iPad with iPadOS installed. Make sure your MacBook Pro, iOS device, or iPadOS device have Wi-Fi and Bluetooth turned on and are signed in with the same Apple ID.

Click to continue what you were doing on your iPhone.

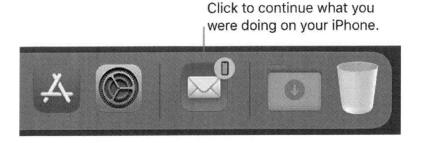

Turn on Handoff on your MacBook Pro. Open System Preferences, click General, then select "Allow Handoff between this Mac and your iCloud devices."

Turn on Handoff on your iOS or iPadOS device. Go to Settings > General > Handoff, then tap to turn on Handoff. If you don't see the option, your device doesn't support Handoff.
Turn on Handoff on your Apple Watch. In the Apple Watch app on iPhone, go to Settings > General, then tap to turn on Enable Handoff.

Handoff works with Safari, Mail, Calendar, Contacts, Maps, Messages, Notes, Reminders, Keynote, Numbers, and Pages.

Use Universal Clipboard on your Mac

Copy content from one device, and paste it to another nearby device within a short period of time. The contents of your clipboard are sent over Wi-Fi and made available to all Mac, iPhone, iPad, and iPod touch devices that are signed in with the same Apple ID and have Handoff, Wi-Fi, and Bluetooth turned on.

Note: To use Universal Clipboard, you need an iPhone or iPod touch with iOS 10 or later, or an iPad with iPadOS installed.

Use across apps. You can copy and paste images, text, photos, and video between any apps that support copy and paste on your Mac, iPhone, iPad, and iPod touch.

Copy and paste files. You can quickly move files from one Mac to another using Universal Clipboard. Copy a file on your MacBook Pro and paste it to a Finder window, Mail message, or any app on a nearby app that supports copy and paste. You must be signed in with the same Apple ID on both computers.

Sidecar on your Mac

With Sidecar, you can turn your iPad into a second display for your Mac and use your iPad as a tablet input device for your Mac apps. Give yourself extra space to work, draw with Apple Pencil, mark up PDFs and screenshots, and more.

Note: You can use Sidecar with iPad models that support Apple Pencil and run iPadOS 13.1 (or later).

Set up and connect. You can use your iPad wirelessly within 32 feet (ten meters) of your Mac, or connect your iPad to your Mac with a cable to keep it charged. To set up your iPad as a second display, go to Apple menu > System Preferences and click Displays, then choose your iPad from the Add Display pop-up menu. Later, you can connect to your iPad in the Display section of Control Center . To disconnect your iPad from your Mac, click the Sidecar button in Control Center. You can also tap in the sidebar of your iPad.

Set Sidecar preferences. To set Sidecar preferences, open System Preferences, then click Displays. Click the name of your iPad, then specify whether you want to use your iPad as the main display or mirror your Mac, show the sidebar and Touch Bar on your iPad and set their locations, and enable double-tap with Apple Pencil to quickly access tools.

Note: If you haven't set up your iPad, you don't see these options in Display preferences.
Extend or mirror your desktop. When you connect your iPad, it automatically becomes an extension of your Mac desktop, so you can drag your apps and documents between your Mac and iPad. To show your Mac screen on both devices (mirror the display), move

your mouse over the Sidecar button in Control Center, click the right arrow that appears above the button, then select Mirror Built-in Retina Display. To extend your desktop again, open the menu and choose Use As Separate Display.
Tip: For quick access to the Sidecar options, you can set Display

preferences 🖥 to always appear in the menu bar. Go to System Preferences > Dock & Menu Bar, click Display in the sidebar on the left, then select Show in Menu Bar. When Sidecar is on and your iPad is connected, the Display icon in the menu bar changes to

▣.

Use Apple Pencil. Precisely draw and create in your favorite pro apps. Just drag the window from your Mac to your iPad and start using Apple Pencil. Or use Apple Pencil to mark up PDFs, screenshots, and images.

Note: Pressure and tilt for Apple Pencil only work in apps with advanced stylus support.

Take advantage of sidebar shortcuts. Use the sidebar on your iPad to quickly reach commonly used buttons and controls. Tap the buttons to undo actions, use keyboard shortcuts, and display or hide the menu bar, Dock, and keyboard.

Use Touch Bar controls—with or without a Touch Bar. For apps that have Touch Bar support, the controls appear at the bottom of the iPad display, whether or not your Mac has a Touch Bar.

Continuity Camera on your Mac

Use your iPhone, iPad, or iPod touch to scan documents or take a picture of something nearby, and it appears instantly on your Mac. Continuity Camera is supported in many apps, including Finder, Mail, Messages, and more.

Note: To use Continuity Camera, you need an iPhone or iPod touch with iOS 12 (or later) or an iPad with iPadOS 13.1 (or later) installed. Make sure your MacBook Pro and iOS or iPadOS device have Wi-Fi and Bluetooth turned on and are signed in with the same Apple ID.

Insert an image or scan. In an app like Mail, Notes, or Messages, click where you want the image to go, choose File (or Insert) > Import From iPhone or iPad, choose "Take Photo" or "Scan Documents," then take the photo or scan the image on your iOS or iPadOS device. You might need to select your iOS or iPadOS device before taking the photo. Tap Use Photo or Keep Scan. You can also tap Retake if you want to try again.

In an app such as Pages, click where you want the image to be inserted, then Control-click, choose "Import image," and take the photo. You might need to select your device before taking the photo.

Note: To take a scan on your iOS or iPadOS device, drag the frame until what you want to show is in the frame, tap Keep Scan, then tap Save. Tap Retake to rescan the content.

The photo or scan appears where you want it in your document.

Continuity Sketch and Continuity Markup on your Mac

With Continuity Sketch, you can use your nearby iPhone or iPad to draw a sketch and instantly insert it into a document on your Mac—for example, in an email, a message, a document, or a note. Or use Continuity Markup to edit a document using your finger on an iOS device or with Apple Pencil on an iPad, and see those markups on your Mac.

Note: To use Continuity Sketch and Continuity Markup, you need an iPhone or iPod touch with iOS 13 (or later) or an iPad with iPadOS 13.1 (or later). Make sure you're signed in with the same Apple ID on all the devices, and that they have Wi-Fi and Bluetooth turned on. Pressure and tilt for Apple Pencil work only in apps with advanced stylus support.

Insert a sketch. In an app like Mail, Notes, or Messages, position the pointer where you want to insert a sketch. Choose File (or Insert) > Import from iPhone or iPad, then choose Add Sketch. On your iOS device or iPad, draw a sketch using your finger or Apple Pencil (on an iPad that supports it), then tap Done. On your Mac, the sketch appears where you positioned the pointer. Depending on where the sketch is inserted, you can mark it up, enlarge it, and so on.

Mark up a document. With Continuity Markup, you can use a nearby iPad ⬚ or iPhone/iPod touch ⬚ to mark up PDFs, screenshots, and images, and see the results on your Mac. Press and hold the Space bar to view the document in Quick Look, then click the device icon. If both devices are nearby, click Annotate ✏️ , then choose a device. The tool may appear highlighted to show your device is connected.

Start writing, drawing, or adding shapes with your finger or Apple Pencil (on an iPad that supports it). See the updates live on your Mac as you make them on your iPad, iPhone, or iPod touch.

Use AirDrop on your Mac

AirDrop makes it easy to share files with nearby Mac, iPhone, iPad, and iPod touch devices. The devices don't need to share the same Apple ID.

Note: AirDrop for iOS or iPadOS requires devices that the device have a Lightning or USB-C connector and iOS 7 (or later) or iPadOS 13.1 (or later). Not all older Macintosh computers support AirDrop.

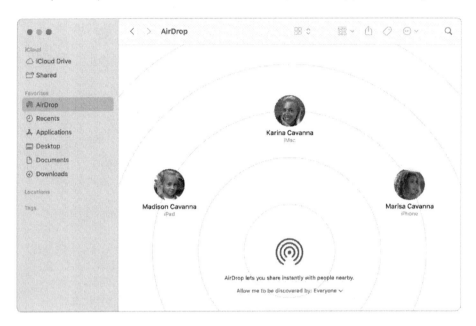

Send a file from the Finder. Control-click the item you want to send, choose Share > AirDrop, then select the device you want to

send the item to. Or click the Finder icon in the Dock, then click AirDrop in the sidebar on the left (or choose Go > AirDrop). When the person you want to send a file to appears in the window, drag the file to them from the desktop or another Finder window. When you send a file to someone, the recipient can choose whether or not to accept the file.

Send a file from an app. While using an app like Pages or Preview,

click the Share button and choose AirDrop, then select the device you want to send the item to.
Control who can send you items using AirDrop. Click the Control

Center icon in the menu bar, click AirDrop , then select "Contacts only" or "Everyone." You can also turn AirDrop on or off here. iPad, iPhone, and iPod touch have similar settings.

86

Tip: If you don't see the recipient in the AirDrop window, make sure both devices have AirDrop and Bluetooth turned on and are within 30 feet (9 meters) of each other. If the recipient is using an older Mac, try clicking "Don't see who you're looking for?"

Receive items using AirDrop. When someone uses AirDrop to send an item to you on your Mac, you can choose whether to accept and save it. When you see the AirDrop notification and want the item, click Accept, then choose to save it to your Downloads folder or an app like Photos. If you're signed in on several devices with the same iCloud account, you can easily send an item (for example, a photo from iPhone) from one device to another, and it's saved automatically.

Share passwords stored in iCloud Keychain. In Safari, you can use AirDrop to share an account password with one of your contacts, or with another Mac, iPhone, iPad, or iPod touch. From the Safari menu, open Preferences > Passwords, select the website whose password you want to share, then Control-click. Choose "Share with AirDrop," then select the person or device in the AirDrop window to share the password.

Phone calls and text messages on your Mac

With a Wi-Fi connection, you can take calls—and make them—right from your MacBook Pro. You can also receive and send text messages.

Set up FaceTime for phone calls. On your iPhone (iOS 9 or later), go to Settings > Phone and enable Wi-Fi calling). Then, on your Mac, go to FaceTime > Preferences, choose Settings, then click "Calls from iPhone."

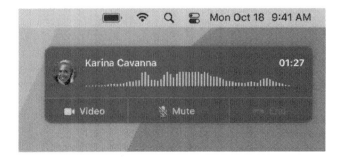

Make a call. Open FaceTime on your Mac and enter a phone number. Or, in Contacts, click the phone icon in the FaceTime row for a contact. You can also click a phone number in a Spotlight search or in an app such as Safari or Calendar (your iPhone or iPad with a cellular connection must be nearby).

Take a call. When someone calls your iPhone, click the notification that appears on your MacBook Pro screen. Your MacBook Pro becomes a speakerphone if you're not wearing headphones.
Tip: To temporarily turn off notifications about phone calls, messages, and more on your Mac, turn on the Do Not Disturb feature. Click the Control Center icon in the menu bar, then click Do Not Disturb and choose a time limit.

Send and receive messages. Use Messages to send text messages from your MacBook Pro. All messages appear on your MacBook Pro, iPhone, iPad, iPod touch, and Apple Watch, so when someone texts you, you can respond with whichever device is closest.

Instant Hotspot on your Mac

Lost your Wi-Fi connection? With Instant Hotspot, you can use the Personal Hotspot on your iPhone or iPad to connect your MacBook Pro to the internet instantly—no password required.

Note: Personal Hotspot requires an iPhone with iOS 8 (or later) or a cellular-model iPad with iPadOS 13.1 (or later).

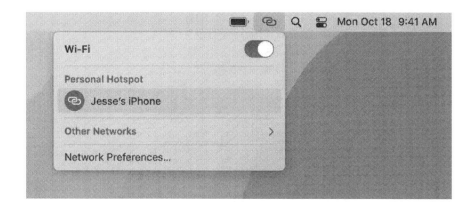

Connect to your device's Personal Hotspot. Click the Wi-Fi status icon 📶 in the menu bar, then click 🔗 next to your iPhone or iPad in the list (if you don't see the list, click Other Networks). The Wi-Fi icon in the toolbar changes to 🔗. You don't need to do anything on your device—MacBook Pro connects automatically. When you're not using the hotspot, your MacBook Pro disconnects to save battery life.

Tip: If you're asked for a password, make sure your devices are set up correctly.

Check the status of your connection. Look in the Wi-Fi status menu to see the strength of the cellular signal.

Unlock your Mac and approve tasks with Apple Watch

When you're wearing your Apple Watch, you can use it to automatically unlock your MacBook Pro and approve authentication tasks—such as entering passwords, unlocking notes and preferences, and authorizing installations—without having to type a password. These features use strong encryption to provide secure communication between your Apple Watch and MacBook Pro.

To use the Auto Unlock and Approve with Apple Watch features:

- Sign in on your Mac and Apple Watch with the same Apple ID.
- Make sure your Apple Watch is unlocked and running watchOS 3 or later to automatically unlock your Mac; approving authentication requests requires watchOS 6 or later.
- Turn on two-factor authentication (see below).

Set up two-factor authentication for your Apple ID. To turn on two-factor authentication, go to Apple menu > System Preferences > Apple ID > Password & Security, then select Set Up Two-Factor Authentication.

Make sure "Disable automatic login" is also selected. (You won't see this option if you're using FileVault, but you can still use the "Auto Unlock" and "Approve with Apple Watch" features.)

Set up Auto Unlock. Sign in on all your devices with the same Apple ID, then open System Preferences on your MacBook Pro. If your Apple Watch has watchOS 6 installed, click Security & Privacy, then click General and select "Use your Apple Watch to unlock apps and your Mac." If your Apple Watch has watchOS 3 to watchOS 5 installed, select "Allow your Apple Watch to unlock your Mac." You can't approve authentication tasks unless you have watchOS 6 or later.

Note: These features work only when your Apple Watch is authenticated with a passcode. You authenticate your Apple Watch each time you put it on, so no extra steps are necessary after you enter your passcode.

Skip the sign-in. Walk up to your sleeping MacBook Pro wearing your authenticated Apple Watch on your wrist, and lift the cover or press a key to wake your MacBook Pro—Apple Watch unlocks it so you can get right to work.

Approve with Apple Watch. If you're prompted for a password, double-click the side button on your Apple Watch to authenticate your password on your Mac. You can view your passwords in Safari, approve app installations, unlock a locked note, and more (requires watchOS 6).

Use Apple Pay on your Mac

You can make easy, secure, and private purchases on websites using Apple Pay on your MacBook Pro. With Apple Pay, your Apple Card and other credit or debit card information is never stored or shared by Apple with the merchant. When you shop online using Safari, look for an Apple Pay checkout option. Confirm payment using your Touch ID, your iPhone or Apple Watch.

Note: Apple Pay and Apple Card aren't available in all countries or regions.

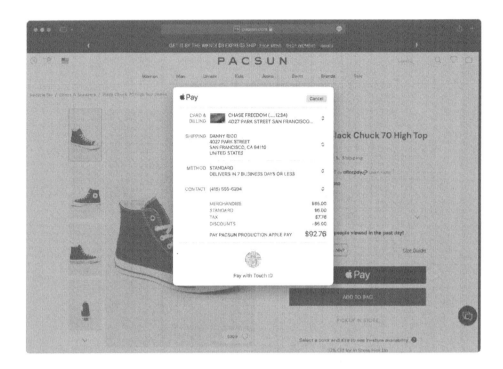

Set up Apple Pay. Apple Pay uses the Apple Card or other credit or debit cards you've already set up on your iPhone or Apple Watch, so no extra setup is required. You must be signed in to an iPhone or Apple Watch that has Apple Pay set up with the same Apple ID you're using on your MacBook Pro. The default payment card, shipping, and contact information that's set on your iPhone or Apple Watch will be used for purchases on your Mac.

Make a purchase using Touch ID. On your MacBook Pro, you're prompted to configure Apple Pay during setup. When you choose Apple Pay on a website, place your finger lightly on the Touch ID sensor to authenticate and complete your purchase.

Make a purchase using the Touch Bar on 13-inch MacBook Pro. When you choose Apple Pay on a website, the merchant name and purchase amount appears on the Touch Bar. Place your finger lightly on the Touch ID sensor to authenticate and complete your purchase.

Make a purchase with iPhone or Apple Watch. Click the Apple Pay button on the website, then to confirm the payment, use Face

92

ID, Touch ID, or the passcode on your iPhone, or double-click the side button on your unlocked Apple Watch. You must be signed in to an iPhone or Apple Watch that has Apple Pay set up with the same Apple ID you're using on your MacBook Pro.

Note: You can add or delete payment cards and manage your Apple Card in the Wallet & Apple Pay pane of System Preferences.

Use AirPlay on your Mac

Show whatever's on your MacBook Pro on the big screen using AirPlay screen mirroring—or use AirPlay to send content to your Mac from an iPhone, iPad, or even another Mac. To mirror the MacBook Pro screen on your TV screen or to use the HDTV as a second display, connect your HDTV to Apple TV and make sure the Apple TV is on the same Wi-Fi network as your MacBook Pro. You can also play web videos directly on your HDTV without showing what's on your desktop—handy when you want to play a movie but keep your work private.

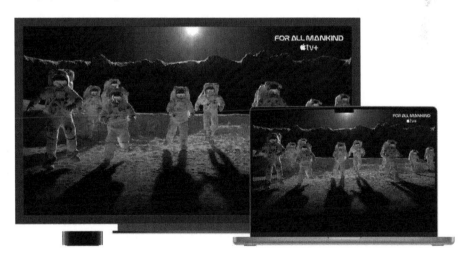

Mirror your desktop using Screen Mirroring. Click the Control Center icon in the menu bar, click Screen Mirroring , then choose your Apple TV. When AirPlay is active, the icon turns blue.

93

Note: If your Mac supports AirPlay screen mirroring, you see an AirPlay status icon in the menu bar of your Mac when an Apple TV is on the same network as your Mac.

In some cases, you can use an AirPlay display even if your MacBook Pro isn't on the same Wi-Fi network as Apple TV (called peer-to-peer AirPlay). To use peer-to-peer AirPlay, you need an Apple TV (3rd generation rev A, model A1469 or later) with tvOS 7.0 or later.

Send content to your Mac from other devices. Watch videos, listen to music, and more on your Mac as they're being played on your other devices. Mirror your iPhone or iPad on your Mac or extend its display by using your Mac as a secondary display for apps that support it, such as Keynote and Photos. Use your Mac as an AirPlay 2 speaker to stream music or podcasts to your Mac, or use it as a secondary speaker for multiroom audio. Your Mac works with any Apple device, and it's even easier to connect if the devices share the same Apple ID.

Play web videos without showing your desktop. When you find a web video with an AirPlay icon ⬆, click the icon, then select your Apple TV.

Tip: If the image doesn't fit your HDTV screen when you mirror the screen, adjust the desktop size for the best picture. Click the AirPlay icon ⬆ in the video, then choose an option under "Match Desktop Size To."
Apple TV is sold separately at apple.com or your local Apple Store.

Use AirPrint on your Mac

If you have an AirPrint-enabled printer, you can print photos and documents from your Mac without having to download and install printer drivers.

You can use AirPrint to print wirelessly to:
  • An AirPrint-enabled printer on your Wi-Fi network

- A network printer or printer shared by another Mac on your Wi-Fi network
- A printer connected to the USB port of an AirPort base station

Print to an AirPrint printer. When you print from an app, click the Printer pop-up menu in the Print dialog, then choose a printer in the Nearby Printers list.

Can't find the printer you're looking for? Make sure it's connected to the same Wi-Fi network as your MacBook Pro. If it's connected and you still don't see it, try adding it: open System Preferences, click Printers & Scanners, then click ✛. (You may have to temporarily connect the printer to your MacBook Pro using a USB cable and, if necessary, an adapter.)

Apps

Apps on your MacBook Pro

Your MacBook Pro comes with a collection of great apps for things you do every day, like browse the web, stay connected with Messages and FaceTime, and manage your calendar. It also comes with apps like Photos, Apple Music, Apple Podcasts, the Apple TV app, Pages, Numbers, and Keynote—so you can be creative and productive right from the start.
Note: Some macOS apps are not available in every region or language.

Where are my apps? You'll find the apps in the Applications folder in your Finder window. You can open apps from the folder or drag them to your Dock. This folder includes a subfolder, Utilities, where you can locate Disk Utility , Keychain Access , Migration Assistant , VoiceOver Utility , and other useful utilities.

Here are some of the apps that come with your Mac. Click the app name to learn more.

Icon	App name
	TV
	Voice Memos
	Safari

	Shortcuts
	Stocks
	Podcasts
	Preview
	Reminders
	Numbers
	Pages
	Photos
	Music

	News
	Notes
	Mail
	Maps
	Messages
	Home
	iMovie
	Keynote
	FaceTime

	Find My
	GarageBand
	App Store
	Books
	Calendar

You'll find additional apps that are not listed in the table above—like

Calculator ▦ , Chess ▦ , Contacts ◆ , TextEdit ▱ , and more—in the Applications folder.

Find even more apps. Click the App Store icon 🅐 in the Dock to find and download apps for almost everything you want to do.

Get help for any app. Click the Help menu (in the menu bar at the top of the screen) when you're using an app.

App Store

Search the App Store to find and download apps, and get the latest updates for your apps.
Find the perfect app. Know exactly what you're looking for? Type the app name in the search field, then press Return. Apps you download from the App Store appear automatically in Launchpad.

You can also find new Safari extensions, which add value to your personal browsing experience, when you click the Categories tab in the sidebar.

Click a tab to browse apps.

Search for an app by name.

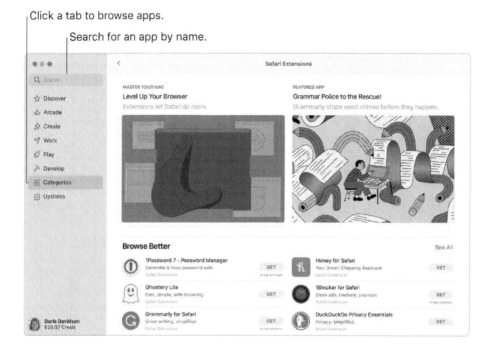

Note: Apple Arcade is not available in all countries or regions.

Ask Siri. Say something like: "Find apps for kids."

All you need is an Apple ID. To download free apps, sign in with your Apple ID—choose Store > Sign In, or click Sign In at the bottom of the sidebar. If you don't have an Apple ID yet, click Sign In, then click Create Apple ID. If you have an Apple ID but don't remember your password, click "Forgot Apple ID or password?" to recover it. You must also set up an account with purchasing information to buy fee-based apps.

Use iPhone and iPad apps on your Mac. Many iPhone and iPad apps now work on your MacBook Pro with Apple silicon. Any available apps that you previously purchased for your iPhone or iPad appear on your Mac. Search for apps in the App Store to see if they're available for Mac.

Game on. Click the Arcade tab to learn how to subscribe to Apple Arcade, discover games you can play, find ones that are popular with your Game Center friends, see your achievement progress, and more. Games you download from the App Store appear automatically in the Games folder in Launchpad, so they're always easy to access, even with a game controller.

Save your game action. You can save up to a 15-second video clip of gameplay by pressing the share button on supported third-party game controllers, so you can review your game strategy or keep a record of memorable gaming moments.

Invite your friends to play. The new multiplayer friend selector makes it easy to invite your recent Messages friends and groups to play Game Center-enabled games. See incoming requests and invitations in the friend request inbox.

Get the latest app updates. If you see a badge on the App Store icon in the Dock, there are updates available. Click the icon to open the App Store, then click Updates in the sidebar.

You have
available updates.

Use the Touch Bar on your 13-inch MacBook Pro. Tap a button to quickly move to the tab you want (Discover, Arcade, Create, Work, Play, Develop, Categories, or Updates).

Books

Use Apple Books to read and organize your library of books and audio books, and to purchase new books on your Mac. Set reading goals and keep track of what you want to read and what you're reading now.

Note: Apple Books is not available in all countries or regions.

A bookshelf on your Mac. Books you've started reading appear at the top in Reading Now. Browse or search all the items in your library—or click Book Store or Audiobook Store in the sidebar and choose a category to find new books and other publications. To buy an item, just sign in with your Apple ID (choose Account > Sign in). You can also buy books right from the search results.

Ask Siri. Say something like: "Find books by Jane Austen."

Type what you're looking for.

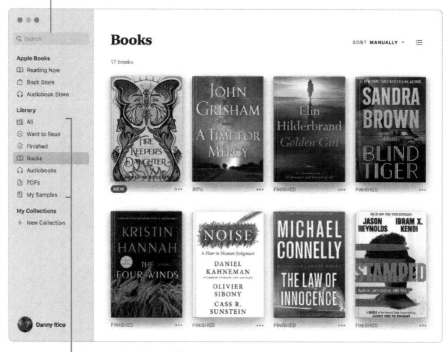

View your books and lists.

Set reading goals. Set daily reading goals to motivate yourself to read more. The default is five minutes a day, but if you want to aim higher, click ⚏ in the Reading Goals section of Reading Now and choose a new goal. You can turn this off and clear reading goal data in Books preferences.

Add bookmarks, notes, and highlights. Move your pointer to the top of the book you're reading to show the controls, then click 🔖 to bookmark a page (click the bookmark again to remove the bookmark). To go to a bookmarked page, show the controls, click 🔖, then click the bookmark. To add notes or highlights, select the text, then choose a highlight color or Add Note from the pop-up menu. To read your notes later, show the controls and click ▤.

Never lose your place or your markups. Your purchased books, collections, bookmarks, highlights and notes, and the current page you're reading are available automatically on your Mac, iOS devices, and iPadOS devices, as long as you're signed in on them with the same Apple ID.

Use the Touch Bar on your 13-inch MacBook Pro. Tap ↺ or ↻ to navigate back or forth in the book, or use the scrubber to move quickly through the pages. Tap 🔍 to search, or tap ⎗ to add a bookmark to the current page.

Tip: Change to Night theme to read more easily in low-light situations. Choose View > Theme, then choose Night, or click the Appearance button AA, then click the black circle. Not all books support Night theme.

Use Night theme.

Calendar

Never miss an appointment with Calendar. Keep track of your busy schedule by creating multiple calendars, and manage them all in one place.

Create events. Click ＋ to add a new event, or double-click anywhere in a day. To invite someone, double-click the event, click the Add Invitees section, then type an email address. Calendar lets you know when your invitees reply.

Ask Siri. Say something like: "Set up a meeting with Mark at nine in the morning."

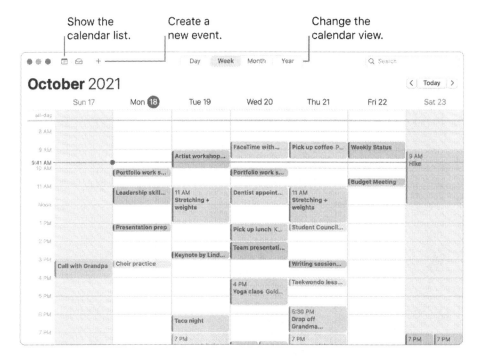

Show the calendar list. Create a new event. Change the calendar view.

Tip: If you add a location to an event, Calendar shows you a map, estimated travel time and time to leave, and even the weather forecast.

A calendar for every part of your life. Create separate calendars—for example, for home, work, and school—each with its own color. Choose File > New Calendar to create a calendar, then Control-click each calendar to choose a new color.

See all your calendars—or just a few. Click the Calendars button to see a list of all your calendars; click the ones you want to see in the window.

Share across your devices and with others. When you're signed in to iCloud, your calendars are kept up to date on all your Macintosh computers, iOS devices, iPadOS devices, and Apple Watch that are signed in with the same Apple ID. You can also share calendars with other iCloud users.

Use the Touch Bar on your 13-inch MacBook Pro. Tap the Today button to view or edit today's events, or use the slider to select the month—past or future.

Select an event in your calendar, and tap buttons to specify the calendar for the event, get event details, edit the time or place, and add or delete invitees.

107

FaceTime

Use FaceTime to make video and audio calls from your Mac to a friend or a group of friends.
Ask Siri. Say something like: "Make a FaceTime call to Sharon."

Make a FaceTime call. Use the built-in FaceTime HD camera on your Mac to make FaceTime video calls. Click New FaceTime, enter a name, phone number, or email address for the person you want to call, then click FaceTime. If it's not convenient to make a video call, click the pop-up menu and select FaceTime Audio to make an audio-only call. When you receive a FaceTime invitation, you can choose to join with video or just audio.

Tip: While a video call is in progress, you can drag the small picture-in-picture window to any corner of the FaceTime window.

List of recent calls

Use FaceTime with a group. You can connect with up to 32 people in a group call. Make a unique link to share with a group. Click Create Link. Copy the link to your Clipboard or share directly with friends in Messages or Mail. You can now use a link to join FaceTime calls on non-Apple devices.

Tip: Add a FaceTime link to a Calendar event to schedule a call for later.

Sign language recognition and Live Captions. FaceTime detects when a participant is using sign language and makes the person prominent in a Group FaceTime call. FaceTime Live Captions detect what's said and present real-time captions for the active speaker.

Make a phone call. If you have an iPhone with iOS 8 or later, make phone calls from your Mac using FaceTime. Just make sure your Mac and iPhone are signed in with the same Apple ID account and that both have the feature turned on. (On your Mac, open FaceTime, choose FaceTime > Preferences, then select "Calls from iPhone.")

Note: Your MacBook Pro and iPhone must be connected to the internet and the same Wi-Fi network to make or receive calls on your Mac.

Use the Touch Bar on your 13-inch MacBook Pro. Start typing a contact's name, then tap your selection. On the Touch Bar, choose Audio or Video for the type of call you want to make.

Find My

Use Find My to locate your friends, family, and Apple devices—all in the same app.

Locate your friends, devices, or items.

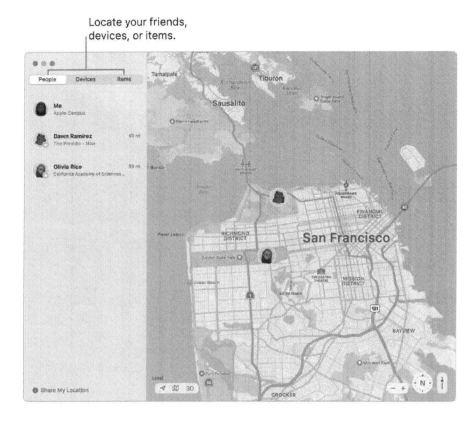

Note: Find My features are not available in all regions or languages.

Share locations with friends. In the People list, click Share My Location to tell friends and family where you are. You can share your live location for an hour, a day, or indefinitely, and stop sharing whenever you like. You can also ask to follow a friend so you can see where they are on a map and get step-by-step directions to their location.

Set location alerts. Automatically send notifications to friends when you arrive at or leave a specific location. Set notifications when your friends leave and arrive, too. If your friends create notifications about your location, you can view them all in one place—click Me in the People list, then scroll to Notifications About You.

Get notified when you leave something behind. Set up separation alerts on your iPhone, iPad, or iPod touch to notify you when you leave your Mac with Apple silicon or another device behind.

Secure a lost device. Use Find My to locate and protect missing devices, like your Mac, iPhone, or AirPods. Click a device in the

Devices list to locate it on the map. Click ⓘ to see options like play a sound on the device to help you find it, mark the device as lost so others can't access your personal information, and even erase the device remotely.

Locate devices, even if they're offline. Find My uses Bluetooth signals from other nearby Apple devices to locate your device when it's not connected to a Wi-Fi or cellular network. These signals are anonymous and encrypted, and help locate your missing device without compromising privacy. You can even find a device that's been erased (for Macintosh computers with macOS 12 or later, iPhones and iPod touch devices with iOS 15 or later, and iPads with iPadOS 15 or later).

Find a family member's device. You can use Find My to help locate a family member's device, if you're in a Family Sharing group and your family member is sharing their location with you.

Find everyday items. Attach an AirTag to an item like your keychain to quickly locate it when you can't find it. Use your iOS or iPadOS device to register an AirTag and compatible third-party items to your Apple ID. To locate items using your Mac, click the Items tab in Find My, then click an item in the list to view its location on the map. If the item can't be located, you can view its last location and receive a notification when the item is found. You can even turn on Lost Mode for an item that includes a message and phone number.

GarageBand

GarageBand is an app for creating, recording, and sharing your music. It has everything you need to learn to play an instrument, write music, or record a song—your own home recording studio.

Create a new project. You can start with a song template, select a tempo, key, and other options, then click Record and start playing. Build your song—for example, with different tracks and loops. Click Quick Help and hold the pointer over items to learn what they are and how they work.

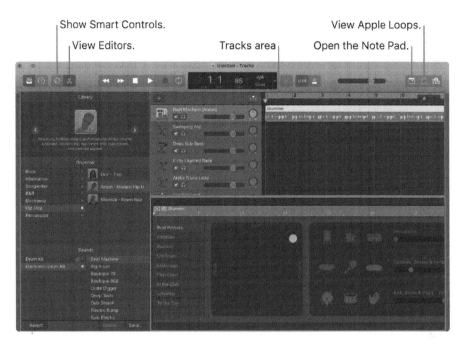

Show Smart Controls.   View Apple Loops.

View Editors.   Tracks area   Open the Note Pad.

Bring in the beat. You can quickly add drums to your project using Drummer Loops. Click the Loop Browser ⬭, then drag a Drummer Loop ▦ into an empty part of the Tracks area. You can customize Drummer Loops to fit your song, using a simple set of controls.

Record your voice. Choose Track > New Track, then select the microphone under Audio. Click the triangle next to Details to set options for input, output, and monitoring, then click Create. Click the Record button ⬤ to start recording, or the Play button ▶ to stop recording.

Click to record your voice.

Choose a track type

| Software Instrument | Audio | Drummer |

Plug in a USB MIDI keyboard to play and record using wide variety of instruments like piano, organ, and synths.

Record using a microphone or line input — or drag and drop audio files.

Connect a guitar or bass to your Mac to play and record through virtual amps and pedal effects.

Add a drummer that automatically plays along with your song.

▼Details:

Input:

◯ Input 1 ◌

☑ I want to hear my instrument as I play and record

My instrument is connected with: Built-in Microphone ⊙

I hear sound from: Built-in Output ⊙

ⓘ

Cancel   Create

Hear yourself while you record.

Use the Touch Bar on your 13-inch MacBook Pro. Easily adjust the Smart Controls for a selected track. Tap buttons to quickly fine-tune the sound of your instrument, turn effects on or off, or adjust the volume of your track.

Home

With the Home app, you can easily and securely control all of your HomeKit accessories from your Mac.

Accessory control. Accessories appear in the Home app as tiles with icons. Click an accessory tile to control it—turn lights on or off, lock or unlock the door, view live cameras, and more. You can also adjust the brightness of a light, or the target temperature of a thermostat. A new visual status at the top of the Home app shows a summary of accessories that need your attention or that have important status changes to share.

Accessories that need your attention appear at the top.

Click an accessory to control it.

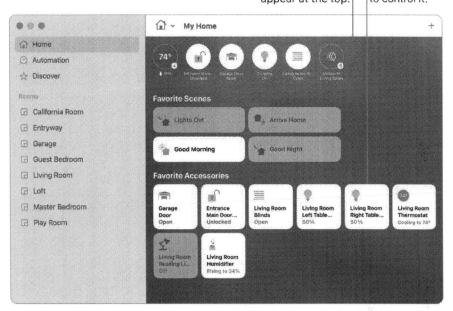

Shared Access. You can share your home with family members or guests, so they can control accessories using the Home app on their own Apple devices.

Create a scene. Create a scene that lets your accessories work together with a single command. For example, make a Good Night scene that turns off all the lights, closes the shades, and locks the door when you turn in for the night. To create a scene, click ✛, then click Add Scene.

HomeKit Secure Video. Connect your home security cameras in the Home app to record your footage and view it from anywhere. It's all end-to-end encrypted, and none of the video counts against your iCloud storage. HomeKit Secure Video requires a supported iCloud plan, compatible HomeKit-enabled security camera, and HomePod, Apple TV, or iPad running as a home hub.

Create activity zones. Define activity zones within a camera's view to capture video or receive notifications only when motion is

115

detected in those areas. In addition to person, animal, package delivery, and vehicle detection, Face Recognition lets security cameras and doorbells identify people you've tagged in the Photos app or in the Home app as recent visitors. (HomeKit Secure Video requires a home hub and a compatible iCloud plan.

Adaptive lighting. Set your smart light bulbs to automatically adjust the color temperature throughout the day to maximize comfort and productivity. Wake up to warm colors, stay focused and alert midday with cooler ones, and wind down at night by removing blue light. (Adaptive lighting requires a home hub.

iMovie

iMovie lets you turn your home videos into beautiful movies and Hollywood-style trailers that you can share with a few quick clicks.

Import a video. Import video from your iPhone, iPad, or iPod touch, from a camera, or from media files already on your Mac. iMovie creates a new library and event for you.

| View your projects. | Correct and adjust color in your clip. | Share a movie, trailer, or clip. |

Record video with the built-in camera. Use the FaceTime HD camera on your Mac to record video and add it to your project. Select an event in the sidebar, click Import in the toolbar, select FaceTime HD Camera, then click the Record button to start and stop recording.

Create Hollywood-style trailers. Make clever trailers, complete with animated graphics and soaring soundtracks. Just add photos and video clips and customize the credits. To get started, click the New button ╈ , click Trailer, choose a template from the Trailer window, then click Create. Add the cast and credits in the Outline tab, and add your own photos and videos in the Storyboard tab.

Click Play to preview the trailer.

Tip: Shooting video with a handheld device can produce shaky results, but you can stabilize the video so the playback is smoother.

Select the clip in the timeline, click the Stabilization button ◀🎥 , then click Stabilize Shaky Video.

Use the Touch Bar on your 13-inch MacBook Pro. Tap to Favorite or Reject any clip in the browser, making it easy to find the clip later or hide it from view. You can also tap in the Touch Bar to play a clip, add a clip to the current movie, or add a clip as a video overlay, such as split screen or picture in picture.

When the timeline is selected, use the Touch Bar buttons to rewind, play, fast-forward, or split the clip into two parts at the point where you click. Tap the volume button in the Control Strip to adjust the volume of a clip.

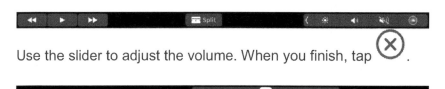

Use the slider to adjust the volume. When you finish, tap ⊗.

Keynote

Create professional, cutting-edge presentations with Keynote. Start with one of the more than 30 predesigned themes and make it your own by adding text, new objects, and changing the color scheme.

Organize visually. Use the slide navigator on the left to quickly add, rearrange, or delete slides. Click a slide to see it in the main window, drag a slide to change its order, or select a slide and press Delete to remove it.

118

Drag to
reorder slides.

Add objects to
your slides.

See format and
animation options.

Practice makes perfect. To rehearse your presentation, choose
Play > Rehearse Slideshow. You'll see each slide along with your
notes—and a clock to keep you on track.

See how you're doing on time.

Remind yourself
of key points to make.

Present in any situation. Present in person using an external display and use your Mac to view upcoming slides, presenter notes, a clock, and a timer. Host a multi-presenter slideshow during a videoconference, and control it as you would when presenting alone. Create an interactive presentation that the viewer controls, control your presentation remotely using your iPhone, iPad, or even your Apple Watch, and more.

Share your presentation. If your manager wants to review your presentation or you want to share it with others on a conference call, choose Share > Send a Copy to send a copy by Mail, Messages, AirDrop, or even social media.

Draw them in. Get their attention by animating an object on a slide. Select the object, click Animate in the toolbar, click Action in the sidebar, then click Add an Effect.

Tip: You can include a video in your presentation. Click where you want it to be, then click the Media button  in the toolbar. Click Movies, then find the movie you want and drag it to your slide.

Use the Touch Bar on your 13-inch MacBook Pro. Tap the arrow buttons to move up or down through your slides. Tap to zoom or skip a slide, or tap to group or ungroup slides. In presentation mode, you see thumbnails of your slides in the Touch Bar.

Mail

Mail lets you manage all your email accounts from a single app. It works with most popular email services, such as iCloud, Gmail, Yahoo Mail, and AOL Mail.

One-stop email. Tired of signing in to multiple websites to check your email accounts? Set up Mail with all your accounts so you can see all your messages in one place. Choose Mail > Add Account.

Ask Siri. Say something like: "Email Laura about the trip."

Find the right message. Type in the search field to see suggestions for messages that best match your query.

Click to search for an item in Mail.

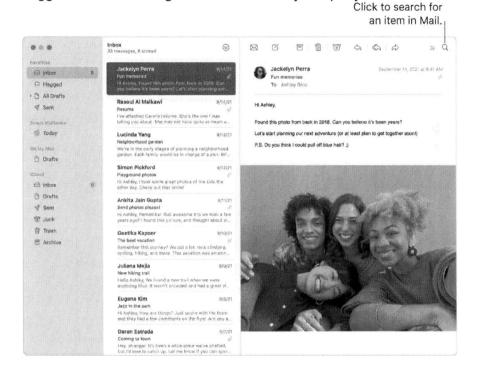

Focus on what's important. See only the messages you want to see in your inbox. You can block messages from specific senders by moving their messages directly to the Trash, mute overly active email threads, and unsubscribe from mailing lists directly in Mail.

Add events and contacts right from Mail. When you receive a message that includes a new email address or event, just click Add in the message to add it to Contacts or Calendar. Force click an address to see a preview of the location, which you can open in Maps.

Protect your privacy. Privacy Protection prevents email senders from learning information about your Mail activity. If you turn it on, it hides your IP address so senders can't link it to your other online activity or determine your location. It also prevents senders from seeing if you've opened their email. Turn it on in Mail Preferences > Privacy, then check Protect Mail Activity.

Translate in a snap. Select the text you want to translate, Control-click the selected text, choose Translate, then choose a language. To translate text you've typed, click "Replace with Translation." You can also download languages so you can work offline—go to the Language & Region pane of System Preferences, then click the Translation Languages button at the bottom. Not all languages are available. Not all languages are available.

Personalize any message. Add emoji or photos with just a click. Select photos from your photo library or take them on iPhone or iPad. You can also add a sketch you've drawn on your iPhone or iPad.

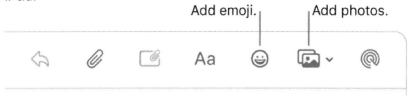

Add emoji.   Add photos.

View in full screen. When you're using Mail in full screen, windows for new messages automatically open in Split View on the right, so it's easy to reference another message in your inbox as you write.

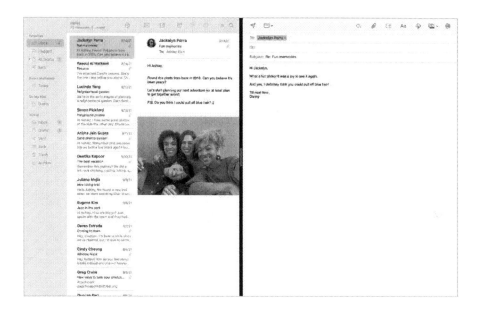

Never miss an email. Check the Mail icon in the Dock to see the number of unread messages. When you get a new email, a notification also appears at the top-right of the screen so you can quickly preview incoming messages. (Don't want notifications? To turn them off, open System Preferences, then click Notifications.)

You have unread messages.

Use the Touch Bar on your 13-inch MacBook Pro. Use the Touch Bar for many common tasks, like composing, replying, archiving, marking as junk, and flagging messages.

Customize the Touch Bar to add your favorite controls (choose View > Customize Touch Bar).

Maps

Get directions and view locations using a map or a satellite image. Get recommendations for the best places to visit in a city, with guides curated by Apple. Force click a location to drop a pin there.

Explore in detail. Maps shows you more details to help you discover what's out there, including landmarks, elevation, natural features, and more. On your Mac with Apple silicon, new city experiences offer details like landmarks, buildings, and even trees.

Plan your route. Use the new driving map to plan your route, check for traffic, and see road details, like turn and bus lanes. Quickly share directions to your iPhone or to a friend via Messages.

Find and save your favorites. Find what you're looking for and filter the results. Click on a place to learn important information, like opening hours for a business or whether a restaurant offers takeout. You can save the places you go most often to your favorites.

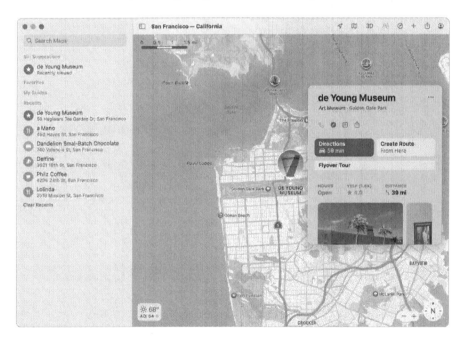

Ask Siri. Say something like: "Find coffee near me."

Discover new places with guides. To help you discover great places around the world to eat, shop, and explore, Maps offers curated guides from trusted brands and partners. You can save these guides and get updates whenever new places are added.

Create your own guides. You can create your own guides for your favorite places and share them with friends and family. To create a guide, move the pointer over My Guides in the sidebar, click ⊕ on the right, then Control-click the new guide to see a menu of options.

Explore in 3D. Click Look Around 👓 to explore select cities in 3D as you move smoothly through the streets in an interactive experience. On your Mac with Apple silicon, you can use the interactive 3D Globe to experience the Earth's natural beauty.

See indoor maps for major destinations. Find your way around select airports and shopping malls. Just zoom in to see what restaurants are near your gate, find a restroom, plan a spot to meet up with friends at the mall, and more.

Open or close the sidebar.

Show your current location.

Show or hide directions.

Get there on public transit. Maps provides Nearby Transit information for select cities, including upcoming departures near you. Click a destination in the sidebar, then click to get suggested travel routes and estimated travel time. Pin your favorite transit lines so they always show up at the top if they're nearby.

EV trip planning made easy. Add your electric vehicle to your iPhone, and Maps shows you where the charging stations are along your route, and accounts for charging times when calculating your ETA.

Plan your cycling route. Maps gives you the info you need to plan your cycling trip, such as elevation, traffic conditions, and whether there are steep inclines. After you plan your trip, you can send it to your iPhone.

Get live ETA updates. When friends and family share their ETA with you, Maps can show you where they are along their route.

Note: Some Maps features are not available in all countries or regions.

Tip: To see what traffic is like, click the View menu in the menu bar, then choose Show Traffic.

Messages

With Messages, it's easy to stay in touch, no matter what device you're using. Manage group texts, pin favorites to the top, easily view content shared with you by others, and much more. You can send text messages to anyone with a Mac, iPhone, iPad, iPod touch, or Apple Watch using iMessage, and send texts to others using SMS/MMS.

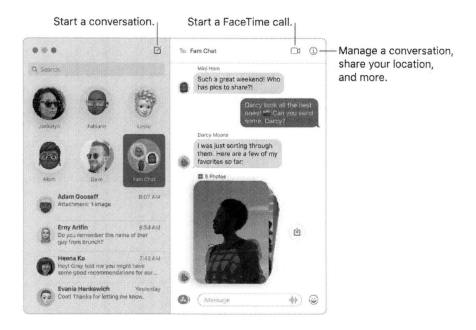

Start a conversation.

Start a FaceTime call.

Manage a conversation, share your location, and more.

Unlimited messages with iMessage. When you sign in with your Apple ID you can exchange unlimited messages—including text, photos, Live Photos, video, and more—with anyone with a Mac, iPhone, iPad, iPod touch, or Apple Watch. The Messages app uses iMessage to send encrypted messages to these devices that appear in blue bubbles in your conversations.

Send SMS/MMS. If you're not using iMessage, you can send and receive SMS and MMS messages on your Mac if your iPhone (with iOS 8.1 or later) is signed in to Messages with the same Apple ID as your Mac. On your iPhone, go to Settings > Messages, tap Text Message Forwarding, then tap the name of your Mac to turn on Text Message Forwarding. On your Mac, you'll see an activation code if you're not using two-factor authentication for your Apple ID. Enter the code on your iPhone, then tap Allow. SMS and MMS messages aren't encrypted and appear in green bubbles in your conversations.

Ask Siri. Say something like: "Message Mom that I'll be late."

Shared with You. Content sent to you over Messages by people in your Contacts automatically appears in a new Shared with You section in the corresponding app, so you can enjoy it when it's convenient for you. Shared with You content appears in Photos,

127

Safari, Apple News, Apple Podcasts, and the Apple TV app. Alongside shared content in the corresponding apps, you can see who sent it, and with a click, open the associated conversation in Messages so you can continue the conversation while you're enjoying what was shared with you.

Keep favorite conversations at the top. Pin your favorite conversations to the top of the messages list by dragging them to the top. New messages, Tapbacks, and typing indicators appear above a pinned conversation. When there are unread messages in a group conversation, the most recent participants appear around the pinned conversation.

Name group conversations.

Pin favorites to the top.

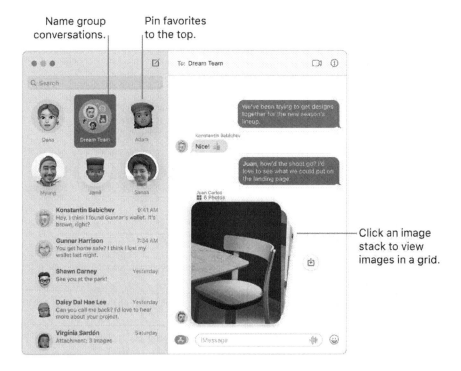

Click an image stack to view images in a grid.

Manage group conversations. Make it easier to identify a group by setting a photo, Memoji, or emoji as the group image. In a group conversation, you can direct a message to an individual by typing the person's name or using the @ sign, and you can respond to a question or statement earlier in the conversation by adding your comment as an inline reply. When a conversation becomes too active, you can hide alerts for the conversation. To set a group

128

image and see options for managing a conversation, select the conversation in the list, then click the Details button (i) in the top-right corner of the Messages window. To receive a notification when you're mentioned, open Messages Preferences, click General, then select the "Notify me when my name is mentioned" checkbox.

Easy photo management. When someone sends you multiple photos, they appear as a collage you can view at a glance. Larger sets are gathered in a stack you can flip through. Click the stack to view the photos as a grid, where you can add a Tapback or inline reply to individual photos. To quickly save a photo to Photos, click the Save Photo button next to it. To see all the photos in a conversation, click the Details button (i).

Make messages fun. Liven up discussions by responding to messages with Memoji stickers, Tapbacks, trending GIFs, or special effects like fluttering confetti, balloons, and more. Messages automatically generates sticker packs based on your Memoji characters. To add a Memoji sticker to a conversation, click the Apps button , click Memoji Stickers, then click the one that best expresses your mood. To add a Tapback, click and hold a message, then choose a Tapback. To add a GIF or special effect, click the Apps button , choose #images or Message Effects, then click the one you want to use. And look out for Digital Touch, invisible ink, and handwritten messages that your friends send you from their iPhone, iPad, or Apple Watch.

Add a photo, sticker, video, or effect.

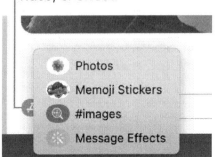

Create your own Memoji. Design your own personalized Memoji— choose skin color and freckles, hairstyle and color, facial features, and more. To use a personalized Memoji as your Messages photo, go to Messages > Preferences. Click "Set up Name and Photo Sharing," click Continue, then click Customize. Click the New Memoji button ⊕, then click each feature to design your look. When you finish, click Done to add the Memoji to your sticker collection. To add more Memoji to your collection, open a conversation, click the Apps button 🅰, click Memoji Stickers, click the New Memoji button ⊕, then have fun designing.

Send a file, photo, or video. Easily share files by dragging them to Messages. Or quickly find and send photos and videos from your Photos library. In a conversation, click the Apps button 🅰, click Photos, then click a photo to add it. Type a keyword—for example, a person's name, date, or location—in the search field to help you find a specific photo.

Share your screen. You and a friend can share screens and even open folders, create documents, and copy files by dragging them to the desktop on the shared screen. Click the Details button ⓘ, then click the Screen Share button ▥.

130

Use the Touch Bar on your 13-inch MacBook Pro. Tap ⬜ to create a new message. Tap the typing suggestions to add words, and tap 😃 to see emoji that you can add to your message. Click a message in the thread to see Tapbacks on the Touch Bar, and tap to add them.

Music

The Apple Music app makes it easy to organize and enjoy your iTunes Store purchases, songs, and albums in your personal library, and in the Apple Music catalog (which lets you listen to millions of songs on demand). Click to view what's next, previously played tracks, and lyrics for what's playing. Shop for the music you want in the iTunes Store.

It's in your library. You can easily view and play your iTunes Store purchases, items you added from the Apple Music catalog, and music in your personal library. Filter your content by Recently Added, Artists, Albums, or Songs.

Browse the best of Apple Music. Click Browse in the sidebar to see new music and exclusive releases from Apple Music, a music streaming service available for a monthly fee. Stream and download more than 50 million songs ad-free, and choose from a large selection of playlists to find the perfect mix for any moment.

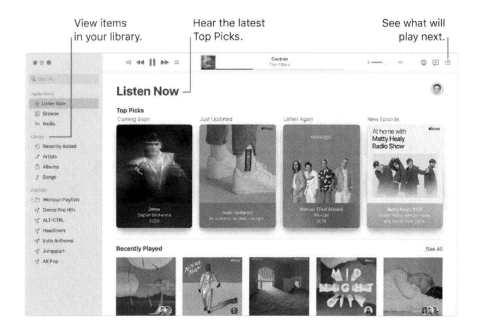

View items in your library.

Hear the latest Top Picks.

See what will play next.

Sing along. Click 💬 in the toolbar to display a panel with lyrics for the current song (if available).

Tune in. Click Radio in the sidebar to tune in to Apple Music 1 live or listen to any episode from the Apple Music family of shows. Explore the variety of stations created for almost every genre of music.

Ask Siri. Say something like: "Add this song to my library." **Sync with ease**. Sync your music content directly in the Apple Music app. When you connect a device, you see it in the sidebar of the Finder. Just drag the content you want onto your device. You can also back up and restore your device in the Finder.

Buy it on the iTunes Store. If you want to own your music, click iTunes Store in the sidebar. (If you don't see the store in the sidebar, choose Music > Preferences, click General, then click Show iTunes Store.)

Tip: When screen real estate is at a premium, switch to MiniPlayer to open a small floating window that you can drag where you want, so you can listen and control your music while doing other things on your Mac. To open MiniPlayer, choose Window > MiniPlayer.

Use the Touch Bar on your 13-inch MacBook Pro. When you're playing a song, you see the rewind, play/pause, and fast-forward buttons in the Touch Bar.

News

Apple News is your one-stop destination for trusted news and information, curated by editors and personalized for you. You can save articles for future reading—even offline or on other devices. Apple News+ lets you read hundreds of magazines, popular newspapers, and premium digital publishers for a single monthly price.

A redesigned news feed in macOS Monterey with more prominent bylines and publication dates makes it easier to browse and verify stories. Save stories right from the news feed to read later or share. News+ subscribers get a more robust search feature and the News+ Library, which organizes your content by magazines, downloaded, newspapers, and catalog—so it's easier to get to your favorites.

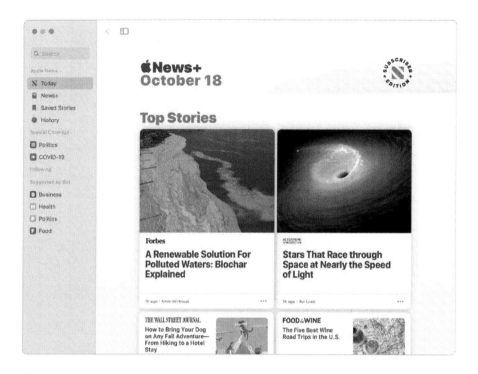

Note: Apple News and Apple News+ are not available in all countries or regions.

Customize your feed. Follow your favorite channels and topics to see them in the Today feed and sidebar. Enter a news outlet or topic in the search field, then click ✛ to follow it.

Tip: If you're reading an article and want to save it for later, choose File > Save Story. To view the article later, click Saved Stories near the top of the sidebar. You can access articles from any of your devices when you sign in with the same Apple ID.

Shared with You. When friends in your contacts share stories with you in Messages, they automatically appear in the new Shared with You section in the Today feed and in the sidebar of Apple News. Stories found in News and Safari appear in Shared with You in both apps—so you can enjoy them in either place.

Use Quick Note to save and organize articles. If you're doing research for a project or upcoming vacation, you can add a Quick Note to a news story and tag it to save it for later. In News, press

Fn-Q or use a specified Hot Corner to open Quick Note and save the article link. You can find the Quick Note later in the sidebar of the Notes app.

Notes

Notes are more than just text. Jot down quick thoughts, or add checklists, images, web links, and more. Add a Quick Note from anywhere—in apps or webpages, on your Desktop, or in full screen or Split View mode. Create and use tags to organize your notes and make it easy to search for notes in the same category. Shared folders let you share an entire folder of notes with a group, and everyone can participate and collaborate. Add mentions (@name) to notes to alert someone to updated content of interest to them. And see all the latest changes in the Activity view.

Ask Siri. Say something like: "Create a new note."

Add a Quick Note from anywhere. With new Quick Note, you can create a note from any app or website on your Mac and view it at any time in the new Quick Notes category in your sidebar. No matter what you're doing on your Mac, you can capture your thoughts, remember a location, or link to a website you want to remember, without having to open Notes. When you return to the original app or website, you see a thumbnail of your Quick Note, reminding you of useful information you noted about that site or app. Tap it to open the Quick Note.

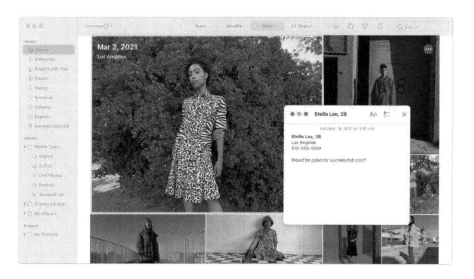

Easy to access. Use the keyboard shortcut Fn-Q or a Hot Corner that you specify in System Preferences 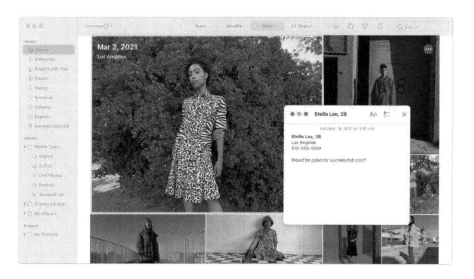 > Desktop & Screen Saver to create a Quick Note wherever you are. In Safari, you can highlight text on a webpage, then click Share > Add Quick Note to add the highlighted text to your note.

Adjust the size or position of your Quick Note (drag a corner to resize the Quick Note or drag the title bar to reposition it), so it doesn't block what you're viewing.

Add content, lock notes, and share them. Use the Notes toolbar to quickly add checklists, photos, videos, sketches, tables, links, and more to your note. Lock your note with a password. Add collaborators to the note, and send a copy of the note using Mail,

Messages, Reminders, or AirDrop.

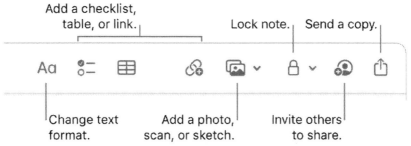

Add a checklist, table, or link.

Lock note.

Send a copy.

Change text format.

Add a photo, scan, or sketch.

Invite others to share.

Tip: When you're signed in with your Apple ID and iCloud is turned on for Notes, your notes are kept up to date on all your devices—so you can create a to-do list on your Mac, then check off items on your iPhone while you're on the go.

Add tags. Use tags anywhere in the body of your note to categorize and organize them. Type the # symbol followed by your tag text. You can view your tags in the sidebar to quickly jump to notes with a specific tag or tags (for example, #vacation or #cooking). Custom Smart Folders automatically collect notes in one place based on the same tags.

Use mentions. Add mentions (type @ followed by a name, for example, @Leslie) to connect directly with your collaborators on a project or in a social setting. They'll get an alert that they've been mentioned in a note, and they can jump right in and participate.

Add tags and mentions.

View the summary of your collaborators' updates.

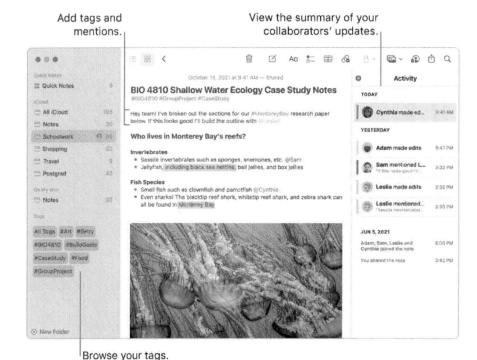

Browse your tags.

View a note's activity summary. See the latest updates about who's been working on a shared note in the Activity view on the right side of the Notes window. Swipe right on note text to view editor callouts showing highlighted changes and the date and time the note was edited.

Customize your toolbar. Control-click anywhere in the tool bar to open the Customize Toolbar window. Drag your favorite items into the toolbar to make it work for you.

Use the Touch Bar on your 13-inch MacBook Pro. Tap ![icon] to create a new note. Tap ![icon] to add a checklist item to your note.

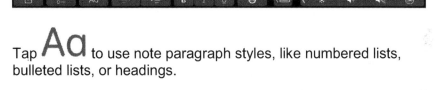

Tap typing suggestions to add text.

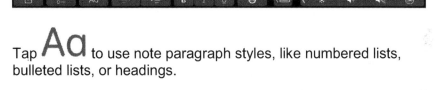

Tap) to display text formatting buttons to align text left or right and apply bold, italic, or underscore styles.

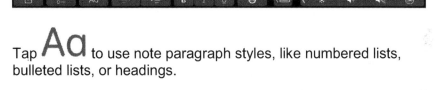

Tap Aa to use note paragraph styles, like numbered lists, bulleted lists, or headings.

Numbers

Use Numbers to create attractive and powerful spreadsheets on your Mac. More than 30 Apple-designed templates give you a head start creating budgets, invoices, team rosters, and more. Numbers can also open and export Microsoft Excel spreadsheets.

Start with a template—then add what you want. Select the sample text in the template, then type new text. To add images, drag a graphic file from your Mac to the placeholder image.

Get organized with sheets. Use multiple sheets or tabs to show different views of your information. For example, use one sheet for your budget, another for a table, and a third for notes. Click ✛ to add a new sheet. Drag a tab left or right to reorder sheets.

Click ✛ to add
a new sheet.

Drag a tab left or right
to reorder sheets.

Formulas are a snap. Get built-in help for more than 250 powerful functions—just type the equal sign (=) in a cell, and you see a list of all the functions and their descriptions in the sidebar. Start typing a formula to get instant suggestions.

Tip: To get instant calculations for a series of values, select the range of cells containing the values. At the bottom of the window you'll see the sum, average, minimum, maximum, and count of the selected values. Click the Menu button 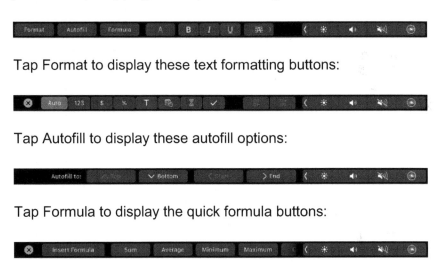 at the bottom right to see even more options.

Create pivot tables. Create a pivot table using a table or range of cells in a spreadsheet as your source data, then use it to analyze any set of data, quickly group and summarize values, and identify interesting patterns and trends. You can edit the cell range of your source data, add and arrange pivot table data, create a snapshot of a pivot table that you can copy to other apps, and more.

Use the Touch Bar with your 13-inch MacBook Pro. Tap Format, Autofill, or Formula to display the options shown below. Tap text style and format buttons to display more options for choosing color, justification, wrapping, and top/bottom alignment for text.

Tap Format to display these text formatting buttons:

Tap Autofill to display these autofill options:

Tap Formula to display the quick formula buttons:

Pages

Use the Pages app to create stunning, media-rich documents and books on your Mac. Open and edit Microsoft Word files, and track changes made by yourself and others.

Look good! Pages includes professional, ready-to-use templates for books, newsletters, reports, résumés, and more, making it easy to start your project.

Add charts, movies, and more.

Open or close the Format sidebar.

All your formatting tools, in one place. Click the Format button

in the toolbar to open the Format inspector. Select something in your document, and the formatting options for it appear.

Flow text around graphics. When you add an image to a text document, the text flows automatically around the image. You can fine-tune how the text wraps in the Format sidebar.

Lore feum quisciliqui ting eugait ullandignim zzrit iriustrud doluptat volum il il iustin utet, sum dolore tat volobor autpat alisim quipis nit iure vendrerit eugait ing et ad magnim amconse min ulla corper in heniat accum am dipit lutatuero od. Aute duisim zzriusto elit illut nismodo uptat, quis am veliquisi. Lor sequis augait lam vel del ullan velis nulputet utat dit nonsed tionsequat.

Lore feum quisciliqui ting eugait ullandignim zzrit iriustrud doluptat volum il il iustin utet, sum dolore tat volobor autpat alisim quipis nit iure vendrerit eugait ing et ad magnim amconse min ulla corper in heniat accum am dipit lutatuero od. Aute duisim zzriusto elit illut nismodo uptat, quis am veliquisi. Lor sequis augait lam vel del ullan velis nulputet utat dit nonsed tionsequat.

Move a graphic into a text block...   **...and the text wraps around the graphic automatically.**

Become a publisher. Pages comes with book templates that let you create interactive books in EPUB format. Add text and images—and even a table of contents. When you're ready, you can make your book available for purchase or download in Apple Books. **Start on your Mac, finish on iPad**. You can keep documents up to date across all your devices when you sign in with the same Apple ID. So you can start composing on one device, and pick up where you left off on another.

Translate in a snap. Select the text you want to translate, Control-click the selected text, choose Translate, then choose a language. To translate the text you've typed, click "Replace with Translation." You can also download languages so you can work offline—go to the Language & Region pane of System Preferences, then click the Translation Languages button at the bottom. Not all languages are available.

Tip: Turn on change tracking to see the changes you and others make to a document. Each person's edits and comments are color-coded, so you can see who made each change. Choose Edit > Track Changes to show the change tracking toolbar.

Use the Touch Bar with your 13-inch MacBook Pro. Tap to

change the paragraph style, and to add typing suggestions. Tap to see more formatting options.

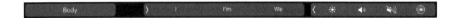

Tap to choose text color, style options (bold, italic, and so on), line spacing, and bullet and list formats. Tap  to return to typing suggestions.

Tap the style (for example, Body) to see other paragraph formatting options, like Title, Subtitle, and Heading. Tap (X) when you finish.

Photos

Use Photos and iCloud Photos to organize, edit, and share your photos and videos, and keep your photo library up to date on all your devices. Photos showcases your best shots, and with more powerful search options, it's easy to find and enjoy your favorites. Easy-to-use editing tools let you transform your photos and videos like a pro.

144

Automatically create
a personalized video
of special moments.

View your photos by
Years, Months, Days,
or All Photos.

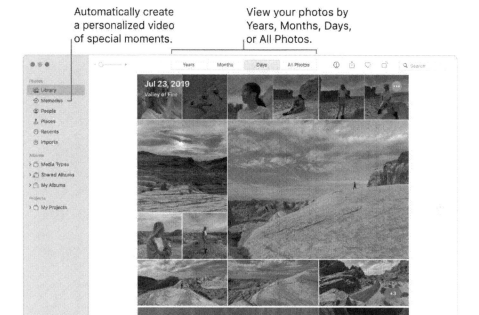

All your photos on all your devices. With iCloud Photos, you can browse, search, and share all the photos and videos from all your devices that are signed in with the same Apple ID. When you take a photo on your iPhone, it's automatically synced with your other devices. And if you edit photos, those edits appear on all of your devices. To get started, open System Preferences, click Apple ID, click iCloud, then select Photos.

Shared with You. When friends in your Contacts send you photos in Messages, they automatically appear in your Photos app, in the Shared with You section. Photos that you're most likely to care about, such as events you attended, appear in your library. When you're viewing the photos in the Photos app, you can click the message bubble on a photo to open Messages and continue the conversation.

Images from Messages appear in Shared with You.

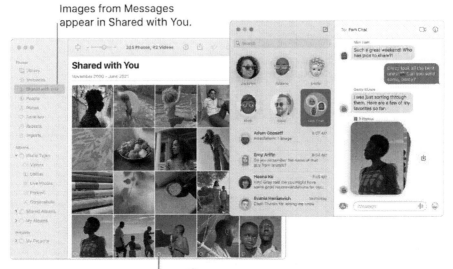

Click ○ to comment in Messages.

Edit like a pro. Create standout photos and videos with powerful but easy-to-use editing tools. Use the editing buttons above your photo or video to improve it with just a click. For more powerful editing tools, click Edit, then use Smart Sliders to get professional results. You can add filters, rotate, increase exposure, and crop both photos and videos.

Interact with text. Live Text recognizes text in images on your computer and on the web. You can copy text from a photo to paste into any file on Mac, or click a phone number or website in the image to call the number or open the website. To translate text, select the text, Control-click it, then click Translate. Not all languages are available.

Relive meaningful moments. Photos highlights important moments like birthdays, anniversaries, and trips. Your photo library comes to life with Live Photos and videos that begin playing as you scroll. Click Memories in the sidebar to have Photos create a memorable movie—complete with music, titles, moods, and transitions—that you can personalize and share. Your Memories are available on all your other devices that use iCloud Photos.

Find what you're looking for. Photos showcases the best shots in your library and hides duplicates, receipts, and screenshots. Click the buttons at the top of the Photos window to view photos by year, month, or day—or click All Photos to quickly view your entire collection. Photos identifies objects, scenes, and people in your photos and videos so you can search your photos based on what's in them, the date they were taken, people you've named in them, captions you added, and their location—if provided. You can also use Spotlight and Siri to search for photos.

Ask Siri. Say something like: "Show me photos of Ursula."

People, places, and things. Visual Lookup recognizes many objects in your photos. Swipe up on a photo or click the information button on a photo to highlight recognized objects and scenes. Learn more about popular art and landmarks around the world, plants and flowers, books, and breeds of pets. To have photos of people important to you always appear at the top of the People album, click the Favorites button ♡ that appears on their photo. Use the Places album to view all your photos with location data on an interactive map. Zoom in on the map to reveal more photos from a specific location.

147

Tip: You can add location info to any photo. While viewing the photo, click the Information button ⓘ , click Assign a Location, and start typing. Choose a location from the list, or type the location and press Return.

Get creative with Live Photos. With Live Photos, use the Loop effect to continuously loop the action, or use Bounce to play the animation forward and backward. For a professional DSLR look, use Long Exposure to blur motion in your Live Photos and turn an ordinary waterfall or flowing stream into a work of art.

Use the Touch Bar with your 13-inch MacBook Pro. The Touch Bar displays a scrubber with all the photos and videos in your library, which you can use to speed your search for just the right photo. You can tap to mark a selected photo as a favorite ♡ , rotate it ⬚ , or add it to a new or existing album.

When you edit a photo, tap buttons to crop, apply filters, adjust light, color, and other settings, or retouch your selection. Use additional options, such as enhance ✦ , compare ■|□ , and more, depending on your selection in the previous Touch Bar.

Podcasts

Use Apple Podcasts to browse, subscribe, and listen to favorite podcasts on your Mac. Personal recommendations help you discover new podcasts grouped by topics you care about.

Get started with Listen Now. See new episodes for the podcasts you're subscribed to, as well as personalized recommendations for podcasts you might be interested in, all in one place. When you're signed in with your Apple ID, any podcasts you're still listening to

148

are saved in Listen Now, even if you started listening on another device.

Ask Siri. Say something like: "Continue playing the last podcast" or "Follow this podcast."

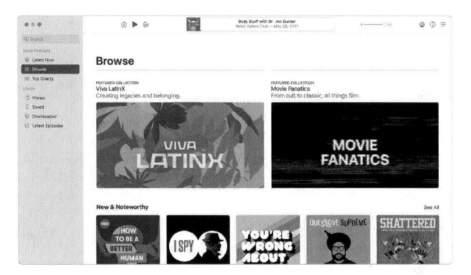

Discover new podcasts. Find topic- and show-based suggestions for new podcasts in Listen Now, or see which shows are trending in Top Charts. If you see a show you like, subscribe to the podcast or add an episode to your library for later. You'll get suggestions for similar topics and shows based on what you enjoy and see the recommendations your friends make in Shared with You.

Shared with You. When friends in your Contacts share podcasts with you in Messages, the episodes automatically appear in the new Shared with You section of Listen Now in Apple Podcasts.

Save episodes to your library. To save a single episode to your library, click ╋ . To keep up with new episodes for an entire podcast, click Subscribe. To download a podcast for offline listening, click ☁️ .

Search by host or guest. When you search for a specific topic or person, you can see results for shows they host, shows that they're a guest on, and even shows where they're mentioned or discussed.

Save ideas with Quick Note. Want to remember a podcast for your next road trip or to listen to while working out? Just create a Quick Note to save the information so you can easily find it later. In Podcasts, press Fn-Q or use a specified Hot Corner to open Quick Note and save the podcast link. You can find the Quick Note later in the sidebar of the Notes app.

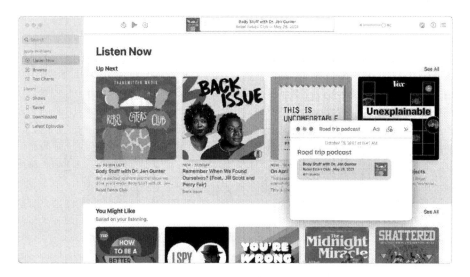

Tip: You can use AirPlay to play a podcast, music, or radio through an external speaker. Click the Control Center icon  in the menu bar, click Screen Mirroring, then select an available speaker.

Use the Touch Bar with your 13-inch MacBook Pro. When you listen to a podcast, use the Touch Bar to pause or resume playing, or move forward or back by sliding the marker on the scrubber bar.

Preview

Use the Preview app to view and make changes to PDFs and images, fill out and sign forms online, annotate PDFs, convert graphic file types, batch edit files, password protect a PDF, highlight and translate text, and much more.

Fill in a PDF form. In Preview, click a field in the form, then type your text. You can choose File > Export to save the form, open it later, and continue to fill it in.

Save a PDF with a password. To secure a PDF, give it a password that users must enter before they can see the contents. In Preview, open the PDF you want to save with a password, choose File > Export, then click Permissions. Select Permissions options, and type a password for Owner Password. Retype it to verify, click Apply, then click Save.
Tip: You can also enter a new name for the PDF before saving to create a copy of the password-secured PDF while keeping the original PDF unencrypted.

Add and remove PDF pages. Open a PDF in Preview and add, delete, or rearrange pages in the PDF:

151

- **Add a page**: Select the page you want to appear before the new page, choose Edit > Insert, then choose "Page from File" or "Blank Page." The new page is inserted after the current page.
- **Delete a page**: Choose View > Thumbnails or View > Contact Sheet, select the page or pages to delete, then press the Delete key on your keyboard (or choose Edit > Delete).
- **Move pages**: Choose View > Thumbnails or View > Contact Sheet, then drag the pages to their new location.
- **Copy a page from one PDF to another**: In each PDF, choose View > Thumbnails or View > Contact Sheet, then drag thumbnail images from one PDF to the other.

Translate in a snap. Select the text you want to translate, Control-click the selected text, choose Translate, then choose a language. You can also download languages so you can work offline—go to the Language & Region pane of System Preferences, then click the Translation Languages button at the bottom. Not all languages are available.

View and convert image files. Preview can convert images to many file types including JPEG, JPEG 2000, PDF, PNG, PSD, TIFF, and others. With the image open in Preview, choose File > Export, click the Format menu, choose a file type, type a new name and choose a location for the file, then click Save. If you don't see the option you want in the Format menu, hold the Option key while you click the menu to view specialized or older formats.

Tip: To convert more than one image file at a time, open the files in one window, select them in that window's sidebar (press Command-A to select all), then follow the steps above. You can also batch resize image files by selecting them all and choosing Tools > Adjust Size.

Reminders

Reminders makes it easier than ever to keep track of all of your to-dos. Create and organize reminders for grocery lists, projects at work, or anything else you want to track. You can also choose when and where to receive reminders. Make groups to assign shared tasks for a project.

Add tags. Add tags to organize your reminders. Click one or more tags in the sidebar to quickly filter reminders.

Create Custom Smart Lists. Smart Lists automatically sort your upcoming reminders based on dates, times, tags, locations, flags, or priority. Create Custom Smart Lists by selecting filters.

Use smart suggestions. Reminders automatically suggests dates, times, and locations for a reminder based on similar reminders you've created in the past.

Smart Lists keep reminders organized.

Add a reminder.

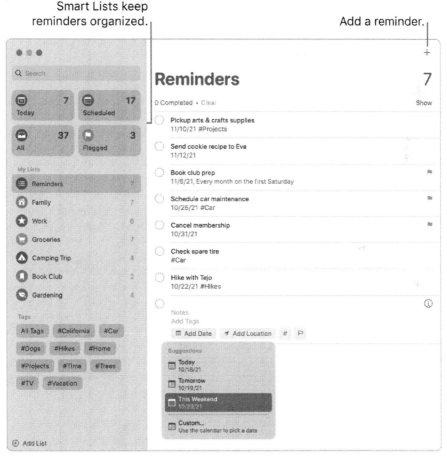

Assign responsibility. Assign reminders to people you share lists with, so that they receive a notification. Split up tasks and make sure everyone knows what they're responsible for. To share a list, choose File > Share List.

Organize with subtasks and groups. To turn a reminder into a subtask, press Command-], or drag it on top of another reminder. The parent reminder becomes bold, and the subtask is indented underneath it. You can collapse or expand your subtasks to keep your view uncluttered.

To group reminders together, choose File > New Group. Name the group whatever you'd like. Add more lists by dragging them into the group, or remove them by dragging them out.
Get reminder suggestions in Mail. When you're corresponding with someone in Mail, you can use Siri to recognize possible reminders and make suggestions for you to create them.
Add a reminder quickly. Use natural language to quickly add a reminder. For example, write "Take Amy to soccer every Wednesday at 5PM" to create a repeating reminder for that day and time.

Ask Siri. Say something like: "Remind me to stop at the grocery store when I leave here."
Use the Touch Bar with your 13-inch MacBook Pro. Use the Touch Bar in Reminders to add new items, check off completed items, flag an item, or add info, time, or location to a reminder.

Safari

Safari is the browser users love for its performance, power-efficiency, and innovative privacy protections. In macOS Monterey, Safari includes redesigned tabs, Tab Groups, a toolbar that matches the color of the site you're browsing, and improved Intelligent Tracking Prevention. The tab bar, extensions, and start page are available across Mac, iPhone, and iPad, so you get the same Safari everywhere you browse, as long as you sign in to iCloud with the same Apple ID.

Start searching. Start typing a word or website address—Safari shows you matching websites, as well as suggested websites. Or select a favorite or frequently visited item from your Safari start page. When you already have a site open, you can type your search criteria in the active tab to launch a new search.

Type what you're looking for.

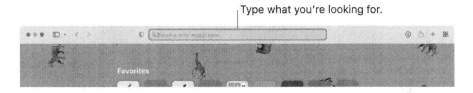

Customize your Safari start page. Your start page can show Favorites, Reading List items, a privacy report, and more. You can import a photo of your own to use as a background image, or choose one of the provided backgrounds. Share your start page across devices. To set options for the start page, click ≡ in the bottom right of the start page.

155

View multiple webpages in one window. Click ✛ at the far right of the tab bar or press Command-T to open a new tab, then enter an address. Tabs resize dynamically as you change the window size. Tabs also pick up the background color of your website.

Hold the pointer over a tab to see a preview of the webpage.

See tab contents quickly. Favicons—icons or logos associated with a website—on tabs let you identify a webpage at a glance. Hold the pointer over a tab to see a preview of the webpage contents.

View the sidebar. Click the Sidebar icon to view the sidebar, where you can manage your Tab Groups, bookmarks, Reading List, and Shared with You links.

Organize with Tab Groups. When you're doing research for a project or vacation, you can open several tabs, then save and

organize them in groups. When the sidebar is open, click the

Add Tab Group icon and choose New Tab Group to create a group from the tabs already open. Or choose New Empty Tab Group and search for tabs to add to a Tab Group. The Tab Groups are saved and visible in the sidebar. Switch between Tab Groups

using the sidebar or the pop-up menu ⌄ if the sidebar is hidden.

Note: Tab Groups are available across devices that are logged into iCloud with the same Apple ID, so you have access to your tabs from anywhere.

Shared with You. When friends in your Contacts share interesting articles, recipes, and other links with you in Messages, they automatically appear in the Shared with You section on the Safari start page and in the sidebar. Stories found in both Safari and News appear in the sidebars of both apps, so you can read them where it's most convenient.

Discover extensions. Extensions add functionality to Safari to personalize your browsing experience. You can find extensions that block ads, find coupons, fix your grammar, and quickly save content from your favorite websites. Choose Safari > Safari Extensions to view the extensions category in the App Store, which features spotlighted Safari extensions and categories (Browse Better, Read with Ease, Top Free Apps, and so on). After you get extensions, turn them on in Safari Preferences. Select the Extensions tab, then click checkboxes to turn on extensions.

Make notes on a webpage. Highlight and make notes directly on a webpage with Quick Note, so your notes will be saved for the next time you visit. Click the Share button 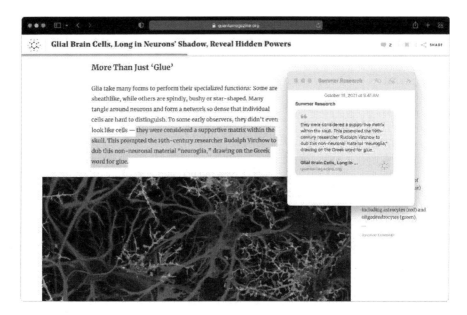 for the webpage and choose Add Quick Note. Open and view saved quick notes from the Notes sidebar or return to the webpage and tap the thumbnail of the saved note to open it.

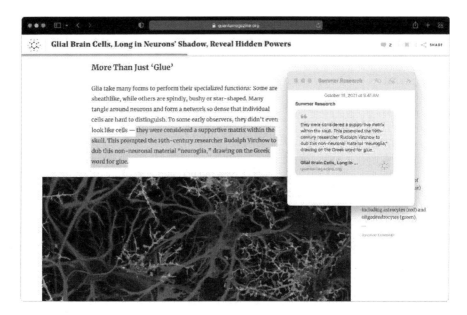

Browse the web safely and privately. Safari automatically upgrades the sites you visit to HTTPS, and warns you when you visit a website that's not secure, or that may be trying to trick you into sharing your personal data. It also protects you from cross-site tracking, by identifying and removing the data that trackers leave behind. Safari asks your permission before letting a social network see what you're doing on third-party sites. And Safari defends you against web tracking by making your Mac harder to identify. Intelligent Tracking Prevention prevents trackers from profiling you using your IP address.

Hide your email address. With an iCloud+ subscription, you can create a unique, random email address any time you need one (for example, when completing a form on a website), with no limit to the number of addresses you can use. When you create a Hide My Email address for a site, any email sent to that address gets forwarded to your personal email account. You can receive email without having to share your actual email address, and you can disable a Hide My Email address at any time.

Use strong passwords. When you sign up for a new account on the web, Safari automatically creates and autofills a new strong password for you. If you choose Use Strong Password, the password is saved to your iCloud Keychain and will autofill on all the devices you log in to with the same Apple ID. Safari securely monitors your passwords, identifying any saved password that may have been involved in a published data breach and making it easy to upgrade to "Sign in with Apple" accounts when available.
View a privacy report. To better understand how a site treats your

privacy, click the Privacy Report button 🛡 to the left of the active tab to view the cross-site trackers that Safari is blocking on each

website. Click ⓘ to see a privacy report with more details about the website's active trackers.

Translate webpages. You can instantly translate entire webpages in Safari. When you encounter a page that Safari can translate, you

see a translate button 🔤 in the website address field. Click to translate between any of the following languages: English, Spanish, Chinese (Simplified), Chinese (Traditional), French, German, Italian, Russian, Brazilian Portuguese, Arabic, Italian, Korean, and

Japanese. The button changes color 🔤 to show when a webpage has been translated.

Note: Translation features are not available in all regions or languages.

Tip: In a webpage, force click a word to see its definition, or a Wikipedia article if one is available. Try force clicking text in other apps, like Messages or Mail, to get more info.
Use the Touch Bar with your 13-inch MacBook Pro. Tap the left or right arrow button in the Touch Bar to go backward or forward. Tap

⊞ to open a new tab.

Tap the tab scrubber in the Touch Bar to move between open tabs.

Tab scrubber

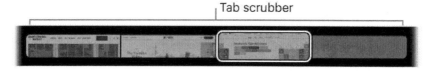

Tap the Search field 🔍 in the Touch Bar, then tap a favorite to open it. When you finish, tap ⊗ to return to the Touch Bar you started with.

Customize the Touch Bar to add your favorite controls (choose View > Customize Touch Bar).

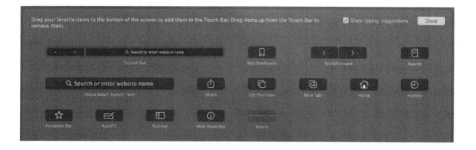

Shortcuts

The Shortcuts app lets you quickly perform multi-step tasks with just a click or by activating Siri. Create shortcuts to get directions to the next event in your Calendar, move text from one app to another, and more. Choose ready-made shortcuts from the Shortcuts Gallery or build your own using different apps to run multiple steps in a task.

View and organize
your shortcuts in
the sidebar.

Click to show
or hide the
sidebar.

View collections
of ready-made
shortcuts.

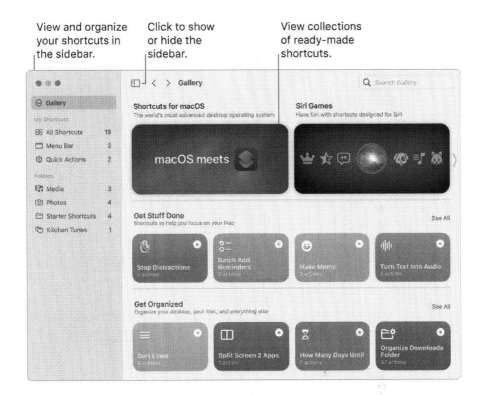

A gallery of possibilities. Browse or search for shortcuts in the Gallery. Starter shortcuts are available for a range of common tasks grouped in collections. The shortcuts you create, and any ready-made shortcuts you choose or edit, are shown in My Shortcuts in the Gallery sidebar. To show or hide the Gallery sidebar, click the Sidebar button ⊞.

Build custom shortcuts. Create a new shortcut, then drag actions from the list on the right to the shortcut editor on the left to produce the result you want. Actions are the building blocks of a shortcut, like steps in a task. Choose from a wide range of actions, such as getting the latest Photo from the Photos app, creating a folder, or copying the current URL from Safari. You can also use actions that run a script, such as rounding a number, setting airplane mode, and doing calculations. Shortcuts also provides "next action" suggestions to help you complete your shortcut.

161

Shortcuts are built with a series of actions.

Click to run the shortcut.

Choose actions in the Action Library.

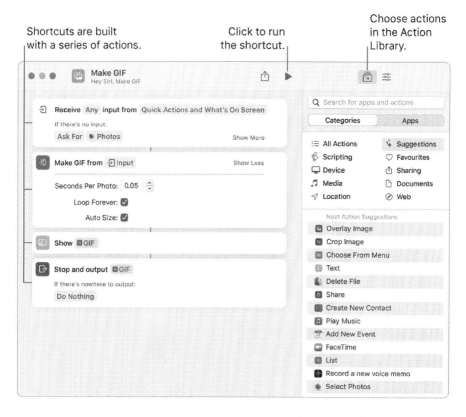

Shortcuts to your shortcuts. Using Siri to run a shortcut is the quickest way to get something done. You can also add shortcuts to the Dock, the menu bar, and the Services menu of apps. Double-click a shortcut, click Shortcut Details 🎚, then choose options under Use as Quick Action.

Ask Siri. Say something like: "Text last image."

Sync and share shortcuts. Sign in to all your devices with the same Apple ID and your shortcuts appear on all of them. Edits you make on one device are automatically reflected on your other devices. You can also share your shortcuts with others and receive shared shortcuts from someone else. To share, double-click the shortcut, click 📤, then choose how you want to share it.

Stocks

The Stocks app is the best way to track the market on your Mac. View prices in the custom watchlist, click a stock to see more details and an interactive chart, and read about what's driving the market, with stories from Apple News.

Click to read the latest business news.

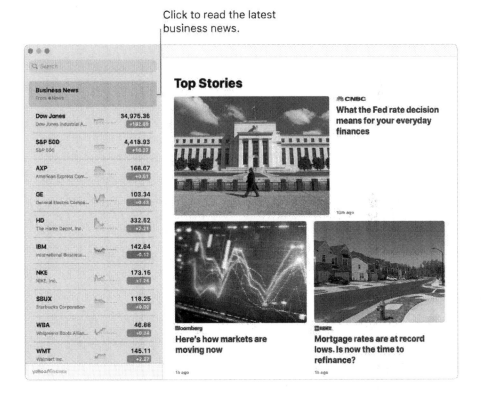

Note: Apple News stories and Top Stories are available in the U.S., Canada, the UK, and Australia. News stories in other countries and regions are provided by Yahoo.

Customize your watchlist. To add a stock to your watchlist, enter a company name or stock symbol in the Search field. In the search results, double-click the stock symbol to view stock information. To add the stock to your watchlist, click the Add to Watchlist button in the top-right corner. To remove a stock, Control-click the stock symbol and choose "Remove from Watchlist." You can also Control-click a stock in your watchlist to open it in a new tab or window.

Check market changes. While viewing your watchlist, click the green or red button below each price to cycle among price change, percentage change, and market capitalization. The watchlist also includes color-coded sparklines that track performance throughout the day.

Read articles related to the companies you follow. Click a stock in your watchlist to see an interactive chart and additional details, and read the latest news about that company. Click Business News at the top of the watchlist to see a collection of timely business articles, curated by Apple News.

Click to cycle between price change, percentage change, and market capitalization.

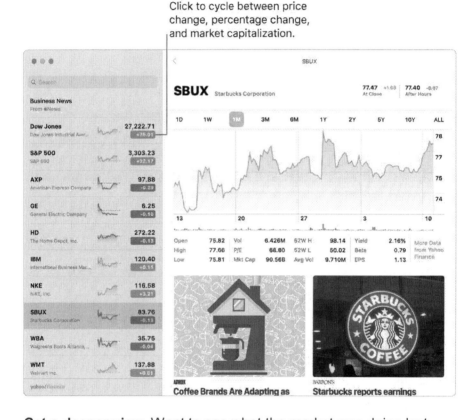

Get a deeper view. Want to see what the market was doing last week, last month, or last year? Click the buttons above the chart to switch timeframes and see prices in the view you like best.

Your watchlist on all your devices. Keep your watchlist consistent across all your devices when you sign in with the same Apple ID.

Tip: For a quick look at the stock market, check the Stocks widget in Notification Center on your Mac.

TV

Watch all your movies and TV shows in the Apple TV app. Buy or rent movies and TV shows, subscribe to channels, and pick up where you left off watching from any of your devices.

Get started with Watch Now. In Watch Now, browse a curated feed of recommendations, based on channels you're subscribed to and movies or TV shows you've watched.

Keep watching in Up Next. In Up Next, you'll find movies or TV shows you're watching, as well as movies and TV shows you've added to your queue. To add a new movie or TV show to Up Next, click the Add to Up Next button.

Discover more in Movies, TV Shows, and Kids. If you're looking for something specific, click the Movies, TV Shows, or Kids tab in the menu bar, then browse by genre.

Buy, rent, or subscribe. When you find a movie or TV show you want to watch, you can choose to buy or rent it. Channels you've subscribed to are available on all devices, and can be used by up to six family members through Family Sharing.

See what your friends are sharing. When your friends and family use the Messages app to share shows and movies with you, you can watch them when it's convenient for you. Just look for them in the Apple TV app—in a new section in Watch Now, called Shared With You. Content only appears in Shared with You if the person who sent it is in your Contacts.

Choose something from your own library. Click Library to see all the movies and TV shows you've purchased or downloaded, organized by genre. To start watching, just click the movie or TV show.

Use the Touch Bar with your 13-inch MacBook Pro. Use the Touch Bar to rewind, pause, or fast-forward what's playing. There's also a scrubber bar for navigating within a TV show or movie and a subtitles button.

Voice Memos

Voice Memos makes it easier than ever to capture personal reminders, class lectures, and even interviews or song ideas. With iCloud, you can access the voice memos you record with your iPhone, right on your MacBook Pro.

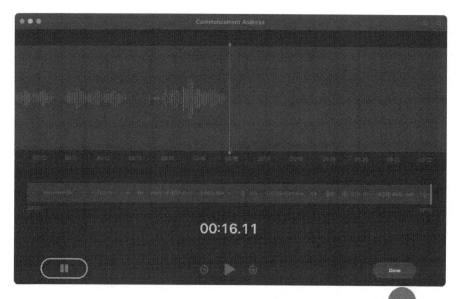

Record from your MacBook Pro. Click the Record button ⬤ to start recording, then click Done to stop. You can rename a recording to make it easier to identify. Click the default name, then enter a

new name. To play back your recording, click the Play button ▶ .

Your voice memos across all your devices. Your voice memos are available on all your devices when you sign in with the same Apple ID. You can access recordings you made with your iPhone or iPad right from your Mac.

Organize with folders. Create folders to help you keep your Voice Memos organized. To add a folder, click the Sidebar button ▥, then click the New Folder button at the bottom of the sidebar. Enter a name for the folder, then click Save. To add a recording to the folder, press and hold the Option key while you drag the recording to the folder.

Mark recordings as Favorites.

Create new folders to organize your recordings.

Mark a recording as a favorite. Select a recording, then click the Favorite button ♡ in the toolbar so you can quickly find the recording later. Click the Sidebar button ▥ to see all your favorites.

Skip silence. Skip over gaps in your audio. Click the Playback Settings button at the top of the Voice Memos window and turn on Skip Silence.

Change the playback speed. Speed up or slow down your audio. Click the Playback Settings button at the top of the Voice Memos window, then drag the slider left or right.

Enhance a recording. Improve the sound quality of your Voice Memos by reducing background noise and room reverberation. Click the Playback Settings button at the top of the Voice Memos window and turn on Enhance Recording.

Use the Touch Bar with your 13-inch MacBook Pro. Use the Touch Bar to record, pause, or play your voice memo.

Find answers

Use the macOS User Guide

The macOS User Guide has a lot more information about how to use your MacBook Pro.

Get help. Click the Finder icon 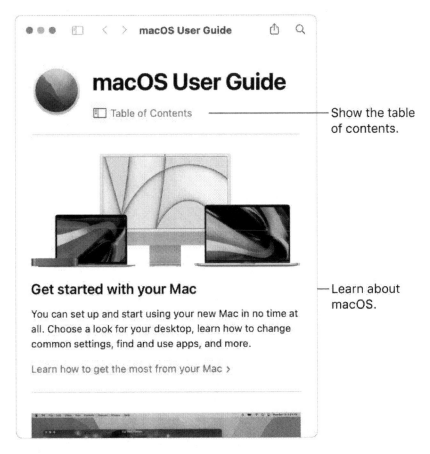 in the Dock, then click the Help menu in the menu bar and choose macOS Help to open the macOS User Guide. Or type a question or term in the search field, then choose a topic from the results list.

Show the table of contents.

Learn about macOS.

Explore topics. To find a topic in the macOS User Guide, you can browse or search. To browse, click "Table of Contents" to see the

169

list of topics, then click a topic to read it. Or type what you want to find in the search field to go right to your answer.

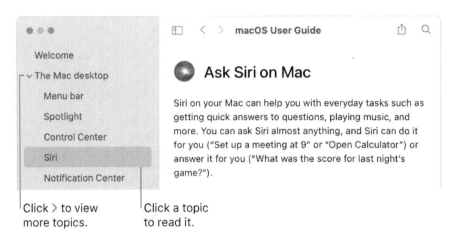

Click > to view more topics.

Click a topic to read it.

Find out what's new. Click the Help menu, then choose "See What's New in macOS" to find out more about the latest features of macOS.

Tip: If you can't remember the location of a menu item in an app, search for it in Help. Place the pointer over the result, and an arrow shows you the command.

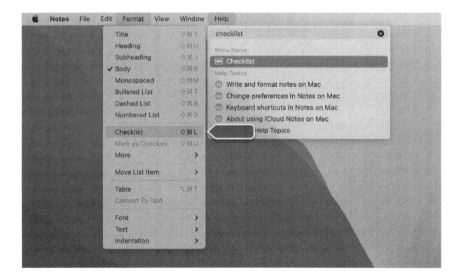

Are you new to Mac?

If this is your first Mac computer, here is some helpful information to get you up to speed—especially if you came from a Windows environment.

Familiarize yourself with the desktop. The desktop is where you do your work, and where you can quickly open apps, search, and organize files.

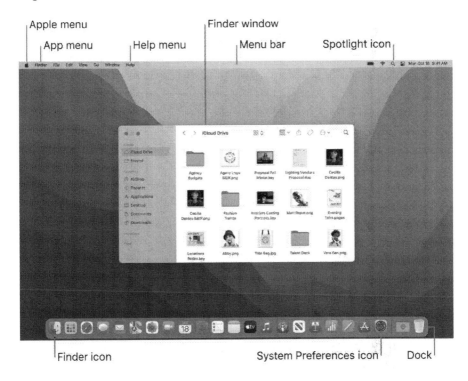

On the desktop you'll find:

- **The menu bar**: The menu bar for the desktop or the active open app is always at the top of the screen. Use menus to find options and perform tasks in apps.
- **The Dock**: The Dock is similar to the taskbar and Start menu in Windows and appears at the bottom of the desktop (but you can change its location in System Preferences). The Dock makes it easy to see all the apps you have open and

171

quickly launch your favorite apps. To open an app, click its icon in the Dock. You can also open apps using Launchpad.

- **The Finder**: Click 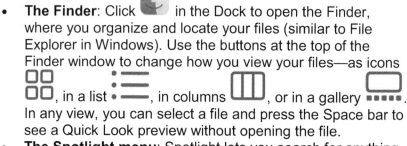 in the Dock to open the Finder, where you organize and locate your files (similar to File Explorer in Windows). Use the buttons at the top of the Finder window to change how you view your files—as icons ⊞, in a list ☰, in columns ⫼, or in a gallery ▪▪▪▪▪. In any view, you can select a file and press the Space bar to see a Quick Look preview without opening the file.
- **The Spotlight menu**: Spotlight lets you search for anything on your Mac, including documents, contacts, email messages, and more. You can also launch apps and search on the web. To open Spotlight, click the Spotlight icon 🔍 at the top right of the screen or press Command-Space bar.

- **System Preferences**: System Preferences ⚙ is similar to the Control Panel in Windows. Customize your Mac with settings for the desktop, Dock, display, Bluetooth, network, and much more.

Get to know the keyboard and trackpad. The Command key ⌘ on Mac is generally the same as the Control key on Windows. For example, use Command-C and Command-V to copy and paste content. The Delete key on Mac is the same as the Backspace key on Windows. Press Fn-Delete to forward delete.

Use the trackpad to click, right-click, force click, scroll, swipe, and resize documents quickly.
Install apps. You can download apps from the App Store or the internet. When you download an app from the internet, you get a disk image file (ending in .dmg) or package file (.pkg). To install the app, locate the .dmg or .pkg file in your Downloads folder, double-click it, then follow the onscreen instructions. You're prompted to delete the disk image or package file after you install the app.

To uninstall an app, find the app in the Applications folder in Finder, then drag the app to the Trash. Some apps have an Uninstaller, which you can use to delete the app and other files associated with it.

Maximize, minimize, and close windows. You can have multiple windows for an app open at a time. Use the buttons in the top-left corner of a window to resize and close windows.

- Click the Close Window button or press Command-W to close the window, but not the app. Press Option-Command-W to close all open windows for the app. Press Command-Q to quit the app.

- Click the Minimize Window button to minimize a window (or press Command-M). Minimizing a window leaves the app open but reduces the window to an icon on the right side of the Dock. Click the icon to restore the window to its previous size.

- Click the Full-Screen Window button to open your app full-screen. To maximize the window, hold the Option key and click the button. Or hover on the button to see more options, such as tiling the window. Press Esc to return the window to its previous size.

Move windows. Drag the window by its title bar to put it where you want it. Some windows can't be moved.

Switch between app windows. Press Command-Tab to quickly switch to the previous app. When you have several app windows open, press and hold Command, then press Tab to see icons for all the open apps. While holding Command, press Tab (or the arrow keys) to move between the apps and select the one you want to be active. Release the Command key to work in the active app.

Take a screenshot. Press Command-Shift-5 to access the Screenshot Utility.

Let Siri do tasks for you. To activate Siri on your 14-inch or 16-inch MacBook Pro, click the Siri icon at the top right of the screen or press the Dictation/Siri key (F5). On your 13-inch MacBook Pro, you can tap the Siri button in the Control Strip on the Touch Bar or press and hold Command-Space bar. If the option is turned on, you can

173

say "Hey Siri" and continue with your request. Ask Siri to open a folder, launch an app, make the screen brighter, and other tasks.

Use your Mac with iPhone, iPad, and Apple Watch. If you sign in to your Apple devices with the same Apple ID, you can easily share files and photos, edit documents, answer email and calls, and send text among devices.

Keyboard shortcuts on your Mac

You can press key combinations to do things on your MacBook Pro that you'd normally do with a trackpad, mouse, or other device. Here's a list of commonly used keyboard shortcuts.

Note: Keyboard shortcuts in apps may vary depending on the language and keyboard layout you're using on your Mac. If the shortcuts below don't work as you expect, look in the app menus in the menu bar to see the correct shortcuts. You can also use the keyboard viewer to see your current keyboard layout, known as an input source.

Shortcut	Description
Command-X	Cut the selected item and copy it to the Clipboard.
Command-C	Copy the selected item to the Clipboard.
Command-V	Paste the contents of the Clipboard into the current document or app.
Command-Z	Undo the previous command. Press Command-Shift-Z to redo.
Command-A	Select all items.
Command-F	Open a Find window, or find items in a document.

Command-G	Find the next occurrence of the item you're searching for. Press Command-Shift-G to find the previous occurrence.
Command-H	Hide the windows of the front app. Press Command-Option-H to view the front app but hide all other apps.
Command-M	Minimize the front window to the Dock. Press Command-Option-M to minimize all windows of the front app.
Command-N	Open a new document or window.
Command-O	Open the selected item, or open a dialog to select a file to open.
Command-P	Print the current document.
Command-S	Save the current document.
Command-W	Close the front window. Press Command-Option-W to close all windows of the app.
Command-Q	Quit the current app.
Command-Option-Esc	Choose an app to Force Quit.
Command-Tab	Switch to the next most recently used app among your open apps.
Command-Shift-5	Open the Screenshot utility. You can also take screenshots using the following shortcuts: • Press Command-Shift-3 to take a screenshot of the entire screen. • Press Command-Shift-4 to take a screenshot of a selected area of the screen. • Press Command-Shift-6 to capture the Touch Bar on the 13-inch MacBook Pro.

Security features on your MacBook Pro

Your MacBook Pro provides security features to protect what's on your computer and prevent unauthorized software apps from loading during startup:

- **Secure storage**: Your MacBook Pro storage drive is encrypted with keys tied to its hardware to provide advanced levels of security. In the event of a catastrophic failure, data recovery may not be possible, so you need to back up your files to an external source.
  You can set up Time Machine or another backup plan to regularly back up your files on the computer.
- **Secure boot and Startup Security Utility**: Support for secure boot is turned on automatically. It's designed to verify that the operating system software loaded on your computer at startup is authorized by Apple.
  If your MacBook Pro doesn't start because it detects an untrusted component, it will start up from a secure recovery partition and automatically correct issues if possible.
- **System integrity**: The MacBook Pro with Apple silicon is designed to verify that the version of macOS software loaded during startup is authorized by Apple, and continues behind the scenes to protect the authorizations established for macOS as it runs. This makes it harder for malware or malicious websites to exploit your Mac.
- **Data Protection**: In addition to the default storage drive encryption in MacBook Pro with Apple silicon, third-party app developers can use file-level encryption to better protect sensitive data, without impacting system performance.

Note: In rare circumstances, such as a power failure during a macOS upgrade, your MacBook Pro may become unresponsive and the firmware on the chip may need to be revived.

Save space on your MacBook Pro

With Optimize Storage, you can automatically free up space on your MacBook Pro by making files available on demand. Your oldest files will be stored in iCloud and on your email IMAP or Exchange server, so you can download them at any time. There are also tools to identify and delete big files.

Optimize storage. To see storage recommendations, go to Apple menu > About This Mac, click Storage, then click Manage. You'll see different recommendations based on how you configured your Mac. If your Mac is low on storage, you'll see an alert with a link to the Storage pane.

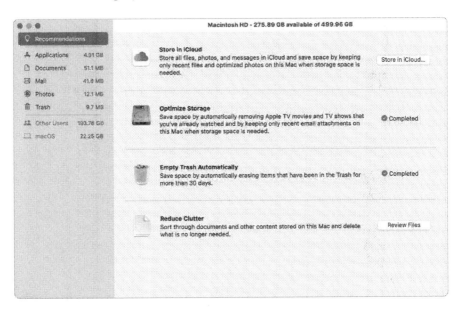

Set options to:

- **Store in iCloud**: Store all files, photos, and messages in iCloud and save space on your Mac.
    - **Desktop and Documents**: Store all the files from your Desktop and Documents folders in iCloud Drive. When storage space is needed, iCloud Drive keeps recently opened files on your Mac and makes your oldest files available on demand.
    - **Photos**: Store photos and videos in iCloud Photos. When storage spaces is needed, iCloud Photos uses optimized versions of photos and video on your Mac and makes the originals available on demand.
    - **Messages**: Store all messages and attachments in iCloud. When storage space is needed, iCloud keeps

177

recent attachments on your Mac and makes your oldest files available on demand.

- Even though your files are stored in the cloud, you can access them right where you left them on your MacBook Pro.
- **Optimize Storage**: Save space on your Mac by optimizing the storage of movies and TV shows in the Apple TV app. You can choose to automatically remove movies or TV shows from your MacBook Pro after you watch them. You can download them again at any time.
- **Empty Trash Automatically**: Automatically erase items that have been in the Trash for more than 30 days.
- **Reduce Clutter**: Easily identify large files, and delete the files you no longer need. To browse large files, click through the categories in the sidebar—Books, Documents, iCloud Drive, Mail, Messages, Music Creation, Photos, Trash, and more.

To help you save space as you work, macOS also:

- Prevents you from downloading the same file twice from Safari
- Alerts you to remove installer software when you finish installing a new app
- Clears logs and caches that are safe to remove when you're low on storage

Take a screenshot on your Mac

Explore the Screenshot menu to find all the controls you need to take screenshots and screen recordings. You can also capture your voice during a screen recording. The optimized workflow lets you take photos and videos of your screen, and then easily share, edit, or save them.

Access the screenshot controls. Press Command-Shift-5. You can capture the entire screen, a selected window, or a portion of a window. You can also record the entire screen or a selected portion of the screen.